BY THE GOLDEN GATE

or

San Francisco, the Queen City of the Pacific Coast;
with Scenes and Incidents Characteristic of its Life

JOSEPH CAREY, D.D.

A Member of the American Historical Association

By the Golden Gate

Joseph Carey

© 1st World Library – Literary Society, 2005
PO Box 2211
Fairfield, IA 52556
www.1stworldlibrary.org
First Edition

LCCN: 2004118270

Softcover ISBN: 1-4218-0462-X
Hardcover ISBN: 1-4218-0362-3
eBook ISBN: 1-4218-0562-6

Purchase *"By the Golden Gate"*
as a traditional bound book at:
www.1stWorldLibrary.org/purchase.asp?ISBN=1-4218-0462-X

1st World Library Literary Society is a nonprofit organization dedicated to promoting literacy by:

- Creating a free internet library accessible from any computer worldwide.
- Hosting writing competitions and offering book publishing scholarships.

Readers interested in supporting literacy through sponsorship, donations or membership please contact:
literacy@1stworldlibrary.org
Check us out at: www.1stworldlibrary.ORG
and start downloading free ebooks today.

By the Golden Gate
contributed by Tim, Ed & Rodney
in support of
1st World Library Literary Society

To My Beloved Wife

this volume

is affectionately inscribed.

CONTENTS

PREFACE 7

CHAPTER I
WESTWARD 9

CHAPTER II
VIEWS FROM THE BOAT ON THE BAY 27

CHAPTER III
SAN FRANCISCO AND THE DISCOVERY OF GOLD 36

CHAPTER IV
THE STORY OF GOLDEN GATE PARK
AND THE CEMETERIES 45

CHAPTER V
THEN AND NOW, OR EIGHTEEN HUNDRED FORTY-
NINE AND NINETEEN HUNDRED AND ONE 56

CHAPTER VI
FROM STREET NOMENCLATURE TO A CANNON 69

CHAPTER VII
CHINAMEN OF SAN FRANCISCO - THEIR CALLINGS
AND CHARACTERISTICS 85

CHAPTER VIII
A CHINESE NEWSPAPER, LITTLE FEET,
AND AN OPIUM-JOINT 98

CHAPTER IX
MUSIC, GAMBLING, EATING, THEATRE-GOING 113

CHAPTER X
THE JOSS-HOUSE, CHINESE IMMIGRATION
AND CHINESE THEOLOGY 127

CHAPTER XI
THE GENERAL CONVENTION OF 1901 139

CHAPTER XII
THROUGH THE CITY TO THE GOLDEN GATE 160

PREFACE

This work now offered to the public owes its origin largely to the following circumstance: On the return of the author from California and the city of Mexico, in November, 1901, his friend, the Rev. John N. Marvin, President of the *Diocesan Press*, asked him to contribute some articles to the *Diocese of Albany*. From these "sketches" of San Francisco this book has taken form. There are chapters in the volume which have not appeared in print hitherto, and such portions as have been already published have been thoroughly revised. Much of the work has been written from copious notes made in San Francisco, and impressions received there naturally give a local colouring to it in its composition.

It is not a history, nor yet is it a guide book; but it is thought that it will be helpful to tourists who visit one of the most picturesque and interesting cities in the United States. It furnishes in a convenient form just such information as the intelligent traveller needs in order to enjoy his walks and rides through the city. The writer in his quest among books could not find any thing exactly of the character here produced; and therefore he is led to give the results of his observations and studies with the hope that the perusal of this volume, sent forth modestly on its errand, will not prove an unprofitable task.

THE AUTHOR.
November 1st, 1902.

CHAPTER I

WESTWARD

Choice of Route - The Ticket - Journey Begun - Pan-American Exposition and President McKinley - The Cattle-Dealer and His Story - Horses - Old Friends - The Father of Waters - Two Noted Cities - Rocky Mountains - A City Almost a Mile High - The Dean and His Anti-tariff Window - Love and Revenge - Garden of the Gods - Haunted House - Grand Canon and Royal Gorge - Arkansas River - In Salt Lake City - A Mormon and His Wives - The Lake - Streets - Tabernacle and Temple - In St. Mark's - Salt Lake Theatre - Impressions - Ogden - Time Sections - Last Spike - Piute Indians - El Dorado - On the Sierras - A Promised Land.

The meeting of the General Convention of the Church in San Francisco, in 1901, gave the writer the long-desired opportunity to visit the Pacific coast and see California, which since the early discoveries, has been associated with adventure and romance. Who is there indeed who would not travel towards the setting sun to feast his eyes on a land so famous for its mineral wealth, its fruits and flowers, and its enchanting scenery from the snowy heights of the Sierras to the waters of the ocean first seen by Balboa in 1513, and navigated successively by Magalhaes and Drake,

Dampier and Anson?

The question, debated for weeks before setting out on the journey, was, which route of travel will I take? It is hard to choose where all are excellent. I asked myself again and again, which line will afford the greatest entertainment and be most advantageous in the study of the country from a historic standpoint? The Canadian Pacific route, and also the Northern Pacific, with their grand mountainous scenery and other attractions, had much to commend them; so also other lines of importance like the Santa Fe with its connecting roads; and the only regret was that one could not travel over them all. But one way had to be selected, and the choice at last fell on the Delaware and Hudson, the Erie, Rock Island, the Denver and Rio Grande, and the Southern Pacific roads. This route was deemed most feasible, and one that would give a special opportunity to pass through cities and places famous in the history of the Nation, which otherwise could not be visited without great expense and consumption of time. It enabled one also to travel through such great States as Pennsylvania, Ohio, Indiana, Illinois, Iowa, Nebraska, Colorado, Utah, and Nevada, as well as central California. As the return journey had also to be determined before leaving home, the writer, desirous of visiting the coast towns of California south of San Francisco, and as far down as San Diego, the first settlement in California by white men, arranged to take the Southern Pacific Railway and the direct lines with which it communicates. In travelling over the "Sunset Route," as the Southern Pacific is styled, he would pass across the southern section of California from Los Angeles, through Arizona, New Mexico, Texas and Louisiana, the line over which President McKinley travelled when he made his tour in the spring of 1901. From New Orleans, by taking the Louisville and Nashville Railroad, he would journey through southern Mississippi, Tennessee, Kentucky, and so back through Ohio from Cincinnati, and across Pennsylvania into the Empire State, over the Erie and the "D. & H." Railways. By the "Sunset Route," too, the writer could avail himself of the privilege of going into the country of Mexico at Eagle Pass, and so down to the City of Mexico, famous with the memories of the Montezumas and of Cortez and furnishing also a memorable chapter in our own history, when, in September 1847, the heights of Chapultepec were stormed by General Pillow and his brave followers.

The journey from beginning to end was one of delightful experiences, full of pleasure and profit, and without a single accident or mishap. This is largely owing to the excellent service afforded and the courtesy of the railway officials, who were ready at all times to answer questions and to promote the comfort of the passengers. The obliging agent of the "D. & H." Railway in Saratoga Springs made all the necessary arrangements for the ticket, with its coupons, which was to take me to and fro; and baggage checked in Saratoga was found promptly, and in good condition, on my arrival in San Francisco. How different our system, in this respect, from that of the English and Continental and Oriental railways! Luggage in those far off countries is a source of constant care, and in Continental Europe and Asiatic lands a heavy item of expense. The old world might learn in several particulars from our efficient American railway system, which has for its prime object facility of travel. The ticket was an object of interest from its length, with its privileges of stopping over at important towns; and strangely, as I travelled down the Pacific coast, with new coupons added, it seemed to grow instead of diminishing. One could not but smile at times at its appearance, and the wonder of more than one conductor on the trains was excited as it was unfolded, and it streamed out like the tail of a kite. It was most generous in its proportions as the railway companies were liberal in their concessions.

It was on September the 23rd, 1901, a bright Monday morning, when I stepped on the "D. & H." for Albany, thence proceeding from the Capital City to Binghamton, where I made connection with the Erie Railway. Travelling on the train with me as far as Albany were Mr. W. Edgar Woolley, proprietor of the Grand Union Hotel, Saratoga, and Mrs. James Amory Moore, of Saratoga and New York city, whose hearty wish that I might have a prosperous journey was prophetic. The country traversed from Saratoga to Binghamton by the "D. & H." Railway affords many beautiful views of hill and valley, and, besides Albany with its long and memorable history and magnificent public buildings and churches, including St. Peter's and All Saints' Cathedral, there are places of note to be seen, such as Howe's Cave and Sharon Springs. By this branch of the "D. & H" system, Cooperstown, rendered famous by James Fenimore Cooper in his works, is reached. On alighting from the train at Binghamton I was greeted by my old friends, Col. Arthur MacArthur, the genial and accomplished editor of the *Troy Budget*, and that witty soul, Rev. Cornelius L. Twing, Rector of Calvary Church, Brooklyn, N.Y., who had come here for the purpose of attending the Annual Conclave of the Grand Commandery of the State of New York. At Buffalo I had sufficient time, before taking the through sleeping car "Sweden," on the Erie Railway, to

Chicago, to visit the Pan-American Exposition grounds. The scene, at night, as I approached, was very impressive. The buildings, illuminated with electricity furnished by the power-house at Niagara's thundering cataract, looked like palaces of gold. The flood of light was a brilliant yellow. The main avenue was broad and attractive. The tower, with the fountains and cascade, appealed wonderfully to the imagination. Machinery, Agricultural, and the Electrical buildings, had an air of grandeur. Music Hall, where the members of Weber's Orchestra from Cincinnati were giving a concert before an audience of three hundred persons, had a melancholy interest for me. It was here, only a short time before, that President McKinley, at a public reception, was stricken down by the hand of an assassin; and the exact spot was pointed out to me by a policeman. In that late hour of the evening, as I stood there rapt in contemplation over the tragic scene which deprived a nation of one of the wisest and best of rulers, I seemed to hear his voice uplifted as in the moment when he was smitten, pleading earnestly with the horrified citizens and officers around him, to have mercy on his murderer, - "Let no one do him harm!" It was Christian, like the Protomartyr; it was the spirit of the Divine Master, Who teaches us to pray for our persecutors and enemies! Happy the nation with such an example before it!

In travelling westward one meets now and then with original and striking characters. They are interesting, too, and you can learn lessons of practical wisdom from them if you will. They will be friendly and communicative if you encourage them. Answering this description was a Mr. H.W. Coffman, a dealer in Short Horn cattle, who was travelling from Buffalo on the Erie road to Chicago. He lives at Willow Grove Stock

Farm, a hundred miles west of Chicago on the Great Western Railway, one mile South of German Valley. Naturally we talked about cows, and we discussed the different breeds of cattle, especially the Buffalo cows of the present-day Egypt, and the Apis of four thousand years ago, which according to the representations, on the monuments, was more like the Devon breed than the Buffalo. The names which he gave to his cows were somewhat poetic. One, for example, was named "Gold Bud;" and another, called "Sweet Violet," owing to her fine build, was sold for $3,705. As the conversation drifted, sometimes into things serious, and then into a lighter vein, Mr. Coffman told a story about a man who had three fine calves. One of them died, and, when his foreman told him, he said he was sorry, but no doubt it was "all for the best." "Skin him," said he, "and sell his hide." Another one died, and he said the same thing. When the last and the best died, his wife said to him, "Now the Lord is punishing you for your meanness!" His reply was, "If the Lord will take it out in calves it is not so bad." I could not but moralise that the Divine judgments on us, for our sins, are not as severe as they might be, and that few of us get what we deserve in the way of punishment or chastening. I also met a horse dealer, who said that he shipped some sixty horses every week to a commission merchant in Buffalo. The latter made three dollars per head for selling them. They brought about $60 a piece. When shipped at New York, by English buyers, for France, South Africa, and elsewhere, they cost about $190 a head. The farmers of Ohio, Indiana, Iowa, and Wisconsin, are getting rich from horse culture and the raising of cattle. He said that fifteen years ago, the farmers, in many instances, had heavy notes discounted in the banks. Now they have no such indebtedness. When formerly he entered a town he would go to a bank and find out from the cashier who had notes there; and then he would go and buy the horses of such men at reduced rates. All is different now. The European demand has helped the American farmer.

At Akron, Ohio, the energetic and successful Rector of St. Paul's Church, the Rev. James H.W. Blake, accompanied by his wife and Miss Graham, his parishioner, boarded the train; and I found them most agreeable travelling companions to San Francisco. In Chicago, in the Rock Island Station, I was met by tourist agent Donaldson, in the employ of the Rock Island Railway Company, and during all the journey he was most courteous and helpful. Here also I found my old classmate in the General Theological Seminary, Rev. Dr. Alfred Brittin Baker, Rector of Trinity Church, Princeton, N.J., Rev. Dr. Henry L. Jones, of Wilkesbarre, Pa., Rev. Dr. A.S. Woodle, of Altoona, Pa., the Rev. Henry S. Foster, of Green Bay, Wis., and the Rev. Wm. B. Thorne, of Marinette, Wis., all journeying to San Francisco. It was a pleasure to see these friends, and to have their delightful companionship.

Many interesting chapters might be written about this journey; and to give all the incidents by the way and descriptions of places visited and pen pictures of persons met would detain you, dear reader, too long, as you are hastening on to the City by the Golden Gate. Some things, however, we may not omit as we travel over great prairies and cross rivers and plains and mountains and valleys. At Rock Island our train crossed the Mississippi, reaching Davenport by one of the finest railway bridges in the country; and as the "Father of Waters" sped on in its course to the Gulf of Mexico, it made one think of the Nile and the long stretches of country through which that ancient river wends its way; but the teeming populations on the banks of the Mississippi have a more noble destiny than the subjects of the Pharaohs who sleep in the necropolis of Sakkarah and among the hills of Thebes and in innumerable tombs elsewhere. They have the splendid civilisation of the Gospel, and they are a mighty force in the growth and stability of this nation, whose mission is worldwide. At Transfer we passed over the Missouri by a long bridge, and entered Omaha, a city picturesquely situated, the home of that doughty churchman, Rev. John Williams, and of Chancellor James M. Woolworth, a noble representative of the laity of the Church. Well may this place be called the "Gate City" of the Antelope State. Towards evening we reached Lincoln, the home of William Jennings Bryan, the Democratic candidate for the presidency in 1896, and also four years later. The house where he lives was pointed out to us. It is a modest structure on the outskirts of the city, comporting with the simplicity of the man himself. In the morning we found ourselves riding over the plains of Colorado. Here are miles and miles of prairie, with great herds of cattle here and there. Here also the eye of the traveller rests on hundreds of miles of snow fences. At last we have our first view of the Rocky Mountains, that great rampart rising up from the plains like huge banks of clouds. It was indeed an imposing view; and it reminded me of the day when, sailing across the sea from Cyprus, I first saw the mountains of Lebanon. You almost feel as if you are going over a sea on this plain, with the Rocky Mountains as an immovable wall to curb it in its tempests. One thought greatly impressed me in the journey thus far, and this is the wonderful agricultural resources of our country. We were travelling over but one belt of the landscape.

Its revelations of fertility, of cultivation, of products, of prosperity, of thrifty homes, of contented peoples, made one feel indeed that this is a land of plenty, and that we are a nation blessed in no ordinary way.

The City of Denver is beautiful for situation, with the Rocky Mountains fifteen miles to the west. As it is on the western border of the great plain, you can hardly at first realise what its elevation is. Yet it is 5,270 feet above the sea, lacking only ten feet of being a mile above tide water. The atmosphere is clear and crisp, and the mountain air exhilarates one in no ordinary degree. Although founded only as far back as 1858, it has to-day a population of 134,000, and it is steadily growing. It has well equipped hotels such as the Palace, the Windsor, the Albany and the St. James. It has also fine public buildings, flourishing churches and schools, and many beautiful homes. There is an air of prosperity everywhere. Here among other places which I visited is Wolfe Hall, a boarding and day school for girls, well equipped for its work, with Miss Margaret Kerr, a grand-daughter of the late Rev. Dr. John Brown, of Newburgh, N.Y., for its principal. I also met the Rev. Dr. H. Martyn Hart, a man of strong personality. I found him in St. John's Cathedral, of which he is the Dean, and of which he is justly proud. It is a churchly edifice, and it suggests some of the architectural form of Sancta Sophia in Constantinople. Dean Hart showed my companions and me what he calls his anti-tariff window. The window was purchased abroad, and the original tariff was to be ten per cent of the cost price. This would be about $75. The window cost $750. Meanwhile the McKinley tariff bill was passed by Congress, and as the duty was greatly increased he would not pay it. Finally the window was sold at auction by the customs' officials, and Dean Hart bought it for $25. As we rode about the city the courteous driver, a Mr. Haney, pointed out a beautiful house embowered in trees, which had a romantic history. A young man of Denver was engaged to be married to a young woman. She jilted him and married another, and while she was on her wedding tour her husband died. The house in which she lived was offered for sale at this juncture, and the original suitor bought it and turned her out into the street. He had his revenge, which shows that human nature is the same the world over. Had he offered her the house to live in, however, it would have been a nobler revenge, "overcoming evil with good."

It is but a short ride from Denver to Colorado Springs, which is a delightful spot with 21,000 inhabitants, and here is a magnificent hotel a block or two from the railway station called the New Antlers. The Rev. Dr. H.H. Messenger, of Summit, Mississippi, an apostolic looking clergyman, with his wife, accompanied us from Denver to Colorado Springs, and also to Manitou, at the foot of Pike's Peak and the mouth of the Ute Pass. From Manitou we drove to the Garden of the Gods, comprising about five hundred acres, and went through this mysterious region with its fantastic and wonderful formations, which seem to caricature men and beasts and to mimic architectural creations. Here we saw the Scotchman, Punch and Judy, the Siamese Twins, the Lion, the elephant, the seal, the bear, the toad, and numerous other creatures. We also viewed the balanced rock, at the entrance, and the Gateway Cliffs, at the northeast end of the Garden, and the Cathedral spires. Everything was indeed startling, and as puzzling as the Sphinx in old Egypt. Nature was certainly in a playful mood when, with her chisel and mallet, she carved these grotesque forms out of stones and rocks.

On the outskirts of Manitou the "Haunted House" was pointed out by the guide, who said that a man and his wife and their son had been murdered here. No one would live in the house now. He asked me if I believed in "Ghosts." I said I was not afraid of dead men, and that I did not think they came back to disturb us. He seemed to agree with me, but hastened to say that he "met a clergyman yesterday who said he believed in them." The house in Manitou which, of all others, interested me most, was the pretty vine-covered cottage of Helen Hunt Jackson, who wrote "Ramona." It was she, who, with a fine appreciation of nature, gave this wild and secluded spot, with its riddles in stone, the suggestive name of "The Garden of the Gods."

At noon on Friday, October 7th, I boarded the Pullman train at Colorado Springs, on the Denver and Rio Grande Railway, for Salt Lake City. On this train was my old friend the Rev. James W. Ashton, Rector of St. Stephen's Church, Olean, N.Y., whom I had not seen for years, and from this hour he was my constant travelling companion for weeks in the California tour, ready for every enterprise and adventure. At Pueblo were some quaint Spanish-looking buildings, and farther on we were among the foothills of the Rocky Mountains. Our train gradually ascended the heights skirting the bank of the Arkansas River, which was tawny and turbid for many a mile. But the Grand Canon of the Arkansas, with its eight miles of granite walls and its Royal Gorge towering nearly three thousand feet above us! It is rightly named. I cannot undertake to describe it accurately. Here are grand cliffs which seemingly reach the heavens, and in some places the rocky walls come so near that they almost touch each other. As you look up, even in midday, the stars twinkle for you in the azure vault. As the train sped on, toiling up the pass through the riven hills and crossing a bridge fastened in the walls of the gorge and spanning the foaming waters, you felt as if you were shut up in the mysterious chambers of these eternal mountains. It is a stupendous work of the Creator, and man dwarfs into littleness in the presence of the majesty of God here manifested as when Elijah stood on Horeb's heights.

It was a pleasant task to study the scenery, wild beyond description at times; and then you would pass upland plains with cattle here and there, and mining camps. That is Leadville, a mile or so yonder to the north; and the children who have come down to the station have valuable specimens of ore in their little baskets, to sell to you for a trifle. Off to the left hand, a little farther on, was a "placer mine," with water pouring out of a conduit, muddy and yellow with "washings." This emptied itself into the Arkansas River, which, from this point down to the foot of the mountains, was as if its bed had been stirred up with all its clay and other deposit. Above this junction the waters of the river were clear and sparkling. It is a picture of life, whose stream is pure and sweet until sin enters it and vitiates its current. Miles beyond are snow sheds, and the famous Tennessee Pass, 10,440 feet above the sea level. This is the great watershed of the Rocky Mountains, and two drops of water from a cloud falling here, - the one on the one side and the other on the other side of the Pass, - are separated forever. One runs to the Atlantic Ocean through rivers to the Gulf of Mexico, and the other to the Pacific Ocean. So there is the parting of the ways in human experience. There are the two ways, and the little turns of life determine your eternal destiny!

Even after a night of travel through the mountains and across the Colorado Desert, we still, in the morning, find our train speeding on amid imposing hills, but now we are in Utah. This we entered at Utah Line. At length we cross the Pass of the Wahsatch Mountains at Soldier Summit, 7,465 feet above the sea, and some thirty miles farther west we enter the picturesque Utah Valley. At length we see the stream of the River Jordan, which is the connecting link between Utah Lake and the Great Salt Lake, and at last we find ourselves in the city founded by Brigham Young and his pioneer followers in 1847. There is a monument of the Mormon prophet in Salt Lake City, commemorating this founding. Standing on the hill above the present city and looking out on the great valley, with his left hand uplifted, he said: "Here we will found an empire!" And here to-day in this city, which bears his marks everywhere, is a population of 54,000 souls, two-thirds of whom profess the Mormon faith.

Here we were met by Bishop Abiel Leonard, D.D., of Salt Lake, who was a most gracious host and who welcomed us with all the warmth of his heart. He had engaged accommodations for us at the Cullen House; and when I went to my room, I looked out on a courtyard bounded on one side by the rear end of a long block of stores. There I saw a wagon which had just been driven into the grounds. Two men were on the seat, the driver and another person, and seated on the floor of the wagon, with their backs toward me, were four women. They wore no hats, as the day was balmy, and I noticed that one had flaxen, another brown, and the two others dark hair. Seeing everything here with a Mormon colouring, I said, "This is a Mormon family. The Mormon farmer has come to town to give his four wives a holiday." It reminded me of similar groups which I had seen in old Cairo, on Fridays, when the Mohammedan went with his wives in the donkey cart to the Mosque. And is there not a strong resemblance between Mormon and Mohammedan? The Mormon husband alighted and gently and affectionately took up one of his wives and carried her into the adjoining store, then a second, and a third. My interest deepened as I watched the proceeding. I said to myself - "How devoted these Mormon husbands, if this is a true example, and how trusting the women!" When he took up the fourth wife to carry her in where her companions were, he turned her face toward me, so that I had a good view of her, and then, to my surprise, nay, amazement, I discovered that she had no feet! But quickly it dawned on my mind, that, instead of real, living Mormon wives, I had been looking on waxen figures, models for show windows! Well, are there not manikins in human life, unreal creatures, who never accomplish more than the models in the windows, who may be looked at, but who perform no noble and lasting deeds?

Our sojourn in Salt Lake City gave ample time to visit the Great Salt Lake, eighty miles long and thirty miles wide, with two principal islands, Antelope and Stansbury; to make a complete study of the city, whose streets run at right angles to each other, with one street straight as an arrow and twenty miles long, and many of them bordered with poplar trees which, as has been facetiously said, were "popular" with Brigham Young; to attend the Saturday afternoon recital on the great organ, in the Tabernacle, which is oval in shape, and has a roof like a turtle's back, and where some three thousand people were assembled; to walk around Temple Square and examine the architecture of the Mormon Temple, which is like a great Cathedral, and into which no one is admitted but the specially initiated and privileged among the Latter-day Saints; to visit many buildings famous in Mormon history, and especially "Zion's Co-operative Mutual Institute," which, in its initials has been said wittily to mean, "Zion's Children Multiply Incessantly;" and on Sunday morning to attend the beautiful service in St. Mark's Church, where Bishop Tuttle, of Missouri, preached a striking sermon from the text "A horse is counted but a vain thing to save a man;" and in the evening to participate in the grand missionary service in Salt Lake Theatre, where the congregation was led by a choir of sixty voices, and stirring addresses were made by Bishop Leonard of Salt Lake, Bishop Gailor of Tennessee, Bishop Jacob, of Newcastle, England, Bishop Dudley, of Kentucky, and Bishop Tuttle, who was formerly Bishop here, before an audience of four thousand people, made up, as the Bishop said, of "Methodists, Presbyterians, Congregationalists, Hebrews, Latter-Day Saints and Churchmen."

What I saw and heard here in Salt Lake City and in other parts of Utah would make a book of itself, but I may say that the only place in which to study Mormonism in all its workings is here in its seat. While polygamy must drop out of the system owing to the laws of the United States, the religious elements will not so soon perish. It has enough of Christianity in it to give it a certain stability like Mohammedanism; but we believe that the Church of the Living God will sooner or later triumph over all forms and teachings which are antagonistic to the Christian Creeds and Apostolic Order. I visited a Mormon bookstore, among other places, and I was amazed at the number of volumes which I found here on the religion of the Latter-Day Saints. In a history of Mormonism, which I opened, was this pregnant sentence - "The pernicious tendency of Luther's doctrine." Surely here is something for reflection!

From Salt Lake City to Ogden, the great centre of railway travel, where several lines converge, is but a ride of thirty-six miles. Here the train, which was very heavy, was divided into two sections, and, after some delay, we went on our journey with hopeful hearts. The Salt Lake Valley and the Great Salt Lake, which we had traced for a long distance, finally disappeared from view. The journey was begun from Ogden on what is known as Pacific time. There are four time sections employed in the United States, adopted for convenience in 1883, - Eastern, Central, Mountain, and Pacific. It is Eastern time until you reach 82-1/2 degrees west longitude from Greenwich, Central time up to 97-1/2, Mountain time till you arrive at 11-1/2, Pacific time to 127-1/2, which will take you out into the Pacific Ocean; and there is just one hour's difference between each time section, covering fifteen degrees. So that when it is twelve o'clock, midday, in New York city, it is eleven in Chicago, ten o'clock in Denver, and nine o'clock in San Francisco. You adapt yourself, however, very readily to these changes of time, in your hours of sleep and in other matters.

One of the places of special interest through which we passed before leaving Utah is Promontory. Here the last tie was laid and here the last spike was driven, on the 10th of May, 1869, when the Central Pacific and the Union Pacific Railways were united and the great cities of the Atlantic seaboard and San Francisco at the setting sun were brought into communication with each other by an iron way which has promoted our civilisation in a marked degree. A night ride over the Alkali Plains of Nevada, famous for their sage brush, was a novelty, and in the clear atmosphere they looked like fields of snow.

At Wadsworth, where our train began to ascend the lower slopes of the Sierra Nevada Mountains, were several Piute Indians. They sell beads, blankets, baskets, and other mementoes. A papoose, all done up in swathing bands, aroused no little curiosity, and when some venturesome passenger with a kodak tried to take a picture of the infant, the mother quickly turned away. They think that the kodak is "the evil eye." There was an old squaw here with whom I conversed, who had a remarkable face on account of its wrinkled condition. She said her name was Marie Martile, and at first she said she was one hundred years old, and later that she was one hundred and fifty. At Reno I saw more Indians with papooses. The thought, however, that this old race is passing away like the fading leaf before the "pale face," is saddening. Soon we arrive in the El Dorado State, we are at last on California soil, and the train with panting engines climbs the dizzy heights of the Sierras, through beautiful forests, along the slopes of hills, through tunnels, beneath long snow sheds. These sheds are a striking feature, and are, with broken intervals, forty miles long. The scenery is remarkable, entirely different from that of the Rocky Mountains; and Donner Lake, into whose clear depths we look from lofty heights, recalls the terrible story of hardship, isolation, suffering and death, here in the winter of 1846 and 1847, when snow-fall on snow-fall cut the elder Donners and several members of this party off from the outside world, and they perished from cold and starvation. Oh, what a tragic, harrowing history it is!

At Summit Station, the loftiest point of the pass over the Sierras, in the path of our railway, engines are changed, and while the train halts passengers amuse themselves by making snowballs. Then we begin the descent along the slopes of the mountains into the great valleys of California. Already we have passed from the region of perpetual snows to a milder clime. We begin to feel the tempered breezes from the Pacific fanning our cheeks. Yes, we are now in the land of a semi-tropical vegetation, a land of beauty and fertility, which in many respects resembles Palestine; and surely it is a Promised Land, rich in God's good gifts. Blue Canon and Cape Horn and beautiful landscapes with vineyards and orange groves are passed, and as night with its sable pall descends upon us, we rest in peace with a feeling of satisfaction and thankfulness to Him Who has led us safely by the way thus far. When the train halted at Sacramento, I had a midnight view of it, and then we sped on to our destination. Some three weeks later, in company with Rev. Dr. Ashton, I visited the valley west of Sacramento, Suisun and Benicia, that I might not lose the view which night had obscured. The Carquinez Straits, with the railway ferryboat "Solano," the largest of its kind in the world, and the upper view of the great Bay of San Francisco, make a deep impression on the mind. I was well repaid for all my pains. But on that first night, as we hastened to our goal, amid landscapes of beauty and fruitfulness traversed in the olden days by the feet of pioneers and gold-seekers, it all seemed as if we were in fairyland. Will the dream be substantial when we enter the City by the Golden Gate?

CHAPTER II

VIEWS FROM THE BOAT ON THE BAY

Arrival at Oakland - "Ticket!" - On the Ferryboat - The City of "Live Oaks" - Mr. Young, a Citizen of Oakland - Distinguished Members of General Convention - Alameda - Berkeley and Its University - Picturesque Scenery - Yerba Buena, Alcatraz and Angel Islands - San Francisco at Last.

It was on the morning of Wednesday, October the second, 1901, when I had my first view of that Queen City of the Pacific coast, San Francisco. Our train, fully nine hours late, in our journey from Salt Lake City, arrived at its destination on the great Oakland pier or mole at 2:30 A.M. The understanding with the conductor the evening before, as we were descending the Sierra Nevada Mountains, was that we would not be disturbed until day break. When the end of our long journey was reached I was oblivious to the world of matter in midnight slumber; but as soon as the wheels of the sleeping coach had ceased to revolve I was aroused with the cry, "Ticket!" First I thought I was dreaming, as I had heard the phrase, "Show your tickets," so often; but the light of "a lantern dimly burning" and a stalwart figure standing before the curtains of my sleeping berth, soon convinced me that I was in a world of reality. This, I may say, was my only experience of the kind, in all my travelling over the Southern Pacific Railway, the Sante Fe, and the Mexican International and Mexican Central Railways. There was little sleep after the interruption; and when the morning came with its interest and novelty I was ready to proceed across the Bay of San Francisco. Our faithful porter, John Williams, whose name is worthy of mention in these pages, as I stepped from the Pullman car, said, "Good-bye, Colonel!" He always addressed me as "Colonel." The porters on all the western roads and on the Mexican railways are polite and obliging, and a word of commendation must be said for them as a class.

The Rev. Dr. James W. Ashton, of Olean, N.Y., my fellow-traveller, and I were soon in the ferry house. We ascended a wide staircase and then found ourselves in a large waiting room, through whose windows I looked out on the Bay of San Francisco for the first time. Off in the distance, in the morning light, I could catch a glimpse of the Golden City of the West. Near by was a departing ferryboat bound for San Francisco. Just then a young man, evidently a stranger, accompanied by a young woman, apparently a bride, accosted me and asked the question, "Sir, do you think we can get on from up here?" Looking at the bay-steamer fast receding, I assured him, somewhat pensively, that I thought we could. In a few moments another steamer appeared in view and speedily entered the dock. The gates of the ferry house were opened and we went on board at once. Most of the passengers at this early hour were those who had come across the Sierras, but there were a few persons from Oakland going over to their places of business in San Francisco. Oakland, so named from the abundance of its live-oaks, has been styled the "Brooklyn" of San Francisco.

It is largely a place of residence for business men, and from fifteen to twenty thousand cross the Bay daily in pursuit of their avocations. It is pleasantly situated on the east side of the Bay, gradually rising up to the terraced hills which skirt it on the east. The streets are regularly laid out and lined with shade trees of tropical luxuriance as well as the live-oaks. Pretty lawns, green and well kept, are in front of many of the houses in the residence part of the city, and here the eye has a continual feast in gazing on flowers in bloom, fuschias, verbenas, geraniums and roses especially. At a later day I visited Oakland, and found it just as beautiful and attractive as it looked in the distance from the deck of the ferry boat. It has several banks, numerous churches, five of our own faith, with some twelve hundred communicants, also good schools, and some fine business blocks. Trolley cars conduct you through its main streets in all directions. Landing at the Oakland pier, one of the largest in the world, and extending out into the Bay some two miles from the shore, the Southern Pacific Railway will soon carry you to the station within the city limits. As you wander hither and thither you see on all sides tokens of prosperity. There is an air of refinement about the place, and you find the atmosphere clear and stimulating. There is not a very marked difference in the temperature of the climate between summer and winter. Frosts are unknown. It is no disparagement to San Francisco to say that Oakland for delicate persons is more desirable. The trade winds as they blow from the Pacific ocean, and make one robust and hardy in San Francisco, when there is vitality to resist them, are tempered as they blow across the Bay some fourteen miles or more, while the fogs, so noted, as they rush in through the Golden Gate and speed onward, are greatly modified as they reach the further shore. As it has such a splendid climate and natural advantages, and enjoys the distinction of being at the terminus of the great overland railway systems, it is constantly attracting to itself population and capital. Ten years ago it had 48,682 inhabitants; to-day it numbers 66,960.

Its people are very hospitable and are glad to welcome the traveller from the east to their comfortable homes. On the ferry boat I was accosted by a ruddy-faced and genial gentleman, a Mr. Young, a resident of Oakland, who was proceeding to his place of business in San Francisco. He gave me some valuable information, and pointed out objects and places of interest. He seemed to be well informed about the General Convention appointed to meet on the day of my arrival, in Trinity church, San Francisco. He spoke with intelligence about its character and purpose, and with enthusiasm concerning its members whom he had met as they were crossing the Bay. The names of Bishop Doane, of Albany, Bishop Potter, of New York, and Mr. J. Pierpont Morgan, were as household words on his lips, and there was a gleam of delight in his eye as he pictured to us the pleasures and surprises in store for us during our sojourn in the Capital of the Golden West.

"That town," said he, "which you see to the south of Oakland, with its long mole, is Alameda. It is a great place of resort, a kind of pleasure grove. Alameda in the Spanish language means 'Poplar Avenue.' Many people go there on excursions and picnic parties from San Francisco, and other places along the Bay. It is, as you see, a very pretty spot. In time it will become a part of Oakland. It has to-day a population of over sixteen thousand people." When I asked him if it had an Episcopal Church, he said, "Yes. Its name is Christ Church, and there are in it four hundred communicants. Do you know its rector? He is the Rev. Thomas James Lacey." Mr. Young, who was a native of Massachusetts and just as proud of California as he was of his old home in the east, turned with considerable elation to Berkeley, the University town. "There," said he, "to the north of Oakland is Berkeley, with a population of thirteen thousand. It is, as you see, situated at the foot of the San Pablo hills, and is about eleven miles from the Market street ferry in San Francisco. To reach it you go by ferry to the Oakland pier and then take the cars on the Southern Pacific road." As I gazed northward, there, as a right arm of Oakland, was the classic town with its aristocratic name, nestling at the foot of the hills in the midst of trees and flowers. It was like a dainty picture with the Bay in the foreground. A nearer view or a visit to it brings the traveller into line with the Golden Gate, through which his eye wanders straight out into the Pacific ocean with all its mystery and grandeur. The University of California was organised by an act of the Legislature in 1868. A law passed then set apart for its work $200,000, proceeds from the sale of tide lands. To this endowment was added the sum of $100,000, from a "Seminary and Public Building Fund." There was also applied to the new university another fund of $120,000, realised from the old college of California, which had been organised in 1855. Then by an act of Congress appropriating 150,000 acres of land for an Agricultural College, which is a part of the equipment of the University, it became still richer. It embraces 250 acres within the area of its beautiful grounds, and so has ample room for expansion. It has departments of Letters, Science, Agriculture, Mechanics, Engineering, Chemistry, Mining, Medicine, Dentistry, Pharmacy, Astronomy and Law. The famous Lick Observatory, stationed on Mount Hamilton near San Jose, is a part of the institution. It has prospered greatly under its present efficient President, Benjamin Ide Wheeler, LL.D.; and it now has three hundred instructors, with over three thousand students. Tuition is free to all students except in the professional departments. It has a splendid library of seventy-three thousand volumes. It will be readily seen that with such an institution of learning, and with the Leland Stanford Jr. University, at Palo Alto, the State of California is giving diligent attention to matters of education. While also there are the various schools and academies and seminaries of the different denominations, it may be said that the church is not backward in this respect. St. Margaret's School for girls, and St. Matthew's School for boys, as well as the Church Divinity School of the Pacific, at San Mateo, where Bishop Nichols resides, and the Irving Institute for girls, and Trinity School in San Francisco, are an evidence of what she is doing for the welfare of the people intellectually, aside from her spiritual ministrations in the dioceses of California and Los Angeles and the Missionary Jurisdiction of Sacramento. Mr. Young was forward to mention the fact that in Berkeley there is the large and influential parish of Saint Mark with a list of nearly four hundred communicants; and this is a great factor for good in the life of such a unique University town. As my eyes turned away from Berkeley, I naturally recalled the great Bishop of Cloyne, after whom the place is named; and as I took into view the wider range of the coast lands, and the blue waters of the magnificent Bay, some fifty miles in length, and, on an average, eight miles wide, and reflected on the significance which attaches to this favoured region, and the influences which go out from this seat of power, and fountain head of riches, I instinctively recalled the noble lines which the eighteenth century prophet wrote when he mused, "On the Prospect of Planting Arts and Learning in America:"

> "Westward the course of empire takes its way;
> The four first acts already past,
> A fifth shall close the drama with the day:
> Time's noblest offspring is the last."

East of us, in picturesqueness, as in a panorama spread out, were the counties of Alameda and Contra Costa, with their receding hills, and Mount Diablo, 3,855 feet in height, lifting up its head proudly. Farther to the south was the rich and beautiful valley of Santa Clara, with its orchards and vineyards. On the west across the Bay were the counties of San Mateo, and San Francisco, with their teeming life, covering a Peninsula twenty-six miles long, and extending up to the Golden Gate; while off to the north, and bordering on the ocean was Marin in its grandeur, crowned with Tamalpais, 2,606 feet above the sea; - and skirting San Pablo Bay was Sonoma with its vine-clad vale. There were the islands of the Bay also, which attracted our attention. Not far from the Oakland pier is Goat Island rising to the height of 340 feet out of the waters, and consisting of 300 acres. It was brown on that October morning when I first saw it, but when the rains come with refreshment in November the islands and all the surrounding country are invested with a robe of emerald green, and flowers spring up to gladden the eyes. Goat Island was so named because goats which were brought in ships from southern ports to San Francisco, for fresh meat, were turned loose here for pasturage for a time; and as these creatures multiplied the island took their name. But it formerly bore the more euphonious title, Yerba Buena, which means in Spanish "Good Herbs." Later in my journeyings to and fro I overheard a lady instructing another person as to the proper way in which to pronounce it, and she made sad work of it. She gave the "B" the sound of the letter G. It also had another name, as you may learn from an old Spanish map of Miguel Costanso, where it is called - Ysla de Mal Abrigo, which means that it afforded poor shelter. It is a government possession, as also the other islands, Alcatraz and Angel. Alcatraz, which Costanso styles, White Island, is smaller than Yerba Buena. In its greatest elevation it is 135 feet above the Bay, and it embraces in its surface about thirty-five acres, about the same area as the Haram Esh-Sherif, or sacred enclosure of the Temple Hill in Jerusalem, with the Mosque of Omar and the Mosque el-Aksa. On its top is a lighthouse, which, on a clear night, sailors can see twelve miles outside of the Golden Gate. Nature, with her wise forethought, seems indeed to have formed this island opposite the Golden Gate, far inside, in the Bay, as a sentinel to watch that pass into the Pacific, and to guide the returning voyager after his perilous journeyings to safe moorings in a land-locked haven. Farther to the north is Ysla de los Angeles, Angel Island, with a varied landscape of hill and plain, comprising some 800 acres of land.

Here are natural springs of water, and in the early days it was well wooded with live-oak trees. To the eyes of Drake and other early navigators and explorers it must have been a vision of beauty, lifting itself out of the waters. Not many trees are seen here now, however, but you may behold instead in harvest time fields of grain. It is especially noted for its stone quarries, and out of these were taken the materials for the fortifications of Alcatraz and Fort Point - as well as the California bank building. It was my privilege at a later day, in company with many of the members of the

General Convention to sail over the Bay and around these islands, which one can never forget. The steamer "Berkeley" was courteously placed at the service of the members of the Convention by the officers of the Southern Pacific Railway; and it was indeed a most enjoyable afternoon under clear and balmy skies as we rode along the shores of the Peninsula, and up the eastern side of the Bay, and northward towards San Pablo, and then around Angel Island and Alcatraz strongly fortified, a distance altogether of forty miles. But now on the first morning, veiled partly with clouds, San Francisco rises on the view, that city of so many memories by the waters of the Pacific, where many a one has been wrecked in body and soul as well as in fortune, while others have grown rich and have led useful lives. Yes, it is San Francisco at last! And while it looms upon the view with its varied landscape, its hills and towered buildings, I am reminded of another October morning when I first saw Constantinople, when old Stamboul with its Seraglio Point, and Galata with its tower, and Pera on the heights above, and Yildiz to the east, and Scutari across the Bosphorus, all were revealed gradually as the mists rolled away. So the Golden City of the West is disclosed to view as the shadows disappear and the clouds break and flee away and the morning sun hastening across the lofty Sierras gilds the homes of the rich and poor alike, and bathes water and land in beauty. There is another city on the shore of a tideless sea, and it will be the joyful morning of eternal life, when, earthly journeys ended, we walk over its golden streets!

CHAPTER III

SAN FRANCISCO AND
THE DISCOVERY OF GOLD

San Francisco - Her Hills - Her Landscapes - Population of Different Decades - The Flag on the Plaza in 1846 - Yerba Buena its Earliest Name - First Englishman and First American to Build Here - The Palace Hotel - The Story of the Discovery of. Gold in 1848 - Sutter and Marshall - The News Spread Abroad - Multitudes Flock to the Gold Mines - San Francisco in 1849.

As we stand on the deck of the bay steamer and are fast approaching the San Francisco ferry-house which looms up before us in dignity, we look out on a great city with a population of 350,000 souls, and we observe that it is seated on hills as well as on lowlands. Rome loved her hills, Corinth had her Acropolis, and Athens, rising out of the Plain of Attica, was not content until she had crowned Mars' Hill with altars and her Acropolis with her Parthenon. Here in this golden city of the Pacific the houses are climbing the hills, nay they have climbed them already and they vie in stateliness with palaces and citadels in the old historic places which give picturesqueness to the coast lands of the Mediterranean. There is indeed in the aspect of San Francisco, in her waters and her skies, and all her surroundings, that which recalls to my mind landscapes and scenery of Italy and Greece and old Syria. Yonder to the northeast of the city is Telegraph Hill, 294 feet high, a spot which in the olden days, that is, as far back only as 1849, was wooded. Now it is teeming with life, and it looks down with seeming satisfaction on miles and miles of streets and warehouses and dwellings of rich and poor. But there are not many poor people in this Queen City. In all my wanderings about the city for a month, I was never accosted by a professional beggar. Everybody could find work to do, and all seemed prosperous and happy. Off to the west, serving as a sentinel, is Russian Hill, 360 feet high. It is a striking feature in the ever-expanding city, and it is a notable landmark for the San Franciscan. In the southeastern part of the city is Rincon Hill, 120 feet in height, attracting to itself the interest of that part of the population whose homes are in its shadow. There are other hills of lesser importance as to altitude, but over their tops extend long streets and broad avenues lined with the dwellings of a contented and thrifty people. The business blocks and hotels, the printing houses and railway and steamship offices, the stores and art galleries, the places of amusement and lecture halls, the stores and shops, the homes and the churches, fill all the spaces between those hills in a compact manner and run around them and stretch beyond them, and at your feet, as you stand on an eminence, is a panorama of life which at once arrests your attention and enchains your mind. It was all so different fifty or sixty years ago. According to the census returns the population of San Francisco in 1850 was 34,000. In 1860 there was a gain of 22,802. In 1870 there were in the city 149,473 souls; while in 1880 there was a population of 233,959 including 30,000 Chinese. The census of 1890 gives an increase of 64,038 during the decade, and the last enumeration shows that there has been a gain of 44,785 in the ten years. If the towns across the bay and northward, as well as San Mateo on the south, which are as much a part of San Francisco as Brooklyn and Staten Island are of New York, there would be a population of more than 450,000. The growth, as will be seen, is steady, and San Francisco offers to such as seek a home within her borders, all the refinements and comforts of life, all that ministers to the intellect and the spiritual side of our nature as well as our social tastes and desires.

There can be no greater contrast imaginable than that between the San Francisco of 1846, when Commodore Montgomery, of the United States sloop of war *Portsmouth*, raised the American flag over it, and the noble city of to-day. And no one then in the band of marines who stood on the Plaza as the flag was unfurled to the breeze by the waters of the Pacific, in sight of the great bay, could have dreamed of the golden future which was awaiting California - of the splendour which would rest on little Yerba Buena in the lapse of time. Yerba Buena was the early name of the settlement. This was applied also, as we have learned, to Goat Island. The pueblo was then insignificant and apparently with no prospect of expansion or grandeur. There were only a few houses there, chiefly of adobe construction, clustering about the Plaza. The Presidio, west of the stray hamlet, and the Mission Dolores, to the southwest, were all that relieved a dreary landscape beyond. There were the hills covered with chaparral and the shifting sands all around, and far to the south, where now are wide streets and great blocks of buildings. The ground sloped towards the bay on the east, and a cove, long since filled in, which bore the name of Yerba Buena, extended up to

Montgomery street. The population of the town was less than a hundred; there was hardly this number in the Presidio, and not more than two hundred people were connected with the Mission Dolores. In 1835 Captain William A. Richardson, an Englishman, the first foreigner to enter the embryo town, erected a tent for his residence; and on July 4th, 1836, the second house was built at the corner of Clay and Dupont streets. The story runs that the first American to build a house in San Francisco proper was Daniel Culwer, who also founded Santa Barbara. This pioneer was born in Maryland in 1793, and died in California in 1857. He lived long enough to see the greatness of the city assured. But on that day when he finished his modest house on the corner of New Montgomery and Market streets, he little thought that in after years there would spring up, as if by magic, under the skillful hands of the Lelands, famous in San Francisco as in Saratoga in the olden days, the magnificent Palace Hotel, with its royal court, its great dining halls, and its seven hundred and fifty-five rooms for guests, rivalling in its grandeur and its luxurious appointments the palaces of kings.

The growth of San Francisco was very rapid after the discovery of gold. The population immediately leaped into the thousands. California was the goal of the gold-seeker, the El Dorado of his quest. Men in search of fortune came from all parts of the world to the Golden West. It was on the 19th of January, 1848, that gold was discovered. The story reads like a romance. Captain John Augustus Sutter, who was born in Baden, Germany, February 15th, 1803, after many adventures in New York, Missouri, New Mexico, the Sandwich Islands, and Sitka, at last found himself in San Francisco. From this spot he crossed the bay and went up the Sacramento River, where he built a stockade, known as Sutter's Fort, and erected a saw mill at a cost of $10,000, and a flour mill at an outlay of $25,000. Here in 1847 he was joined by James Wilson Marshall, born in New Jersey in 1812. Marshall was sent up to the North Fork of the American River, where at Coloma he built a saw mill. This was near the center of El Dorado county, and in a line northeast from San Francisco. The mill, in the midst of a lumber region, was finished on January 15th, 1848, and everything was in readiness for the sawing of timber, which was in great demand in all the coast towns and brought a high price. The mill-race, when the water was let into it, was found too shallow, and in order to deepen it Marshall opened the flood gates and allowed a strong, steady volume of water to flow through it all night. Nature, aided by human sagacity, having done her work well, the flood gates were closed, and there in the gravel beneath the shallow stream lay several yellow objects like pebbles. They aroused curiosity. The miller took one and hammered it on a stone. He found it was gold. He then gave one of the "yellow pebbles" to a Mrs. Wimmer, of his camp, to be boiled in saleratus water. She threw it into a kettle of boiling soap, and after several hours it came out bright and shining. It is yellow gold, California gold, there can be no mistake! Next, we see Marshall, all excitement, hastening to Sutter's Fort, and informing his employer, in a mysterious way, that he has found gold. Sutter goes to the mill the next day, and Marshall is impatiently waiting for him. More water is turned on, and the race is ploughed deeper, and more nuggets are brought to light. It is a day of supreme joy. The excitement is great. Even the waters of the American River seem to "clap their hands" and the trees of the wood wave their tops in homage and rejoice. At the foot of the Sierras is the hidden treasure, which will thrill the civilised world when it hears the tidings with a new joy, which will bring delight beyond measure to thousands of adventurers, which will enrich some beyond their wildest dreams, and which will prove the ruin of many an one, wrecking, alas! both soul and body. Sutler's plan was to keep the wonderful discovery a secret, but this was impossible. Even the very birds of the air would carry the news afar to the coast in their songs; the waters of mountain streams running down to the Sacramento River and on to San Francisco Bay and out to the Pacific Ocean through the Golden Gate would bear the report north and south to all the cities and towns, to Central and South America, to China and Japan, to Europe and more distant lands; and the wings of the wind would serve as couriers to waft the story across the Sierras and the Rocky Mountains and the plains, till the whole world would be startled and gladdened with the cry, Gold is found, gold in California! One of the women of Sutler's household told the secret, which was too big to be kept in hiding, to a teamster, and he, overjoyed, in turn told it to Merchant Smith and Merchant Brannan of the Fort. The "secret" was out in brief space, and like an eagle with outspread wings, it flew away into all quarters of the globe. Poor Sutter, strange to say, it ruined him. The gold seekers came from the ends of the earth and "squatted" on his lands, and he spent all the fortune he had amassed in trying to dispossess them. But his efforts were unavailing. The laws, loosely administered then, seemed to be against him, and fate, relentless fate, spared him not. Almost all that was left to him in the end was the ring which he had made out of the lumps of the first gold found, and on which was inscribed this legend: "The first gold found in California, January, 1848." It tells a melancholy as well as a joyous tale, in it are bound up histories and tragedies, in it the happiness of multitudes, and even the fate of immortal souls! The California legislature at length took pity on Sutter, and granted him a pension of $250 per month, on which he lived until he was summoned, at Washington, D.C., on June 17th, 1880, by the Angel of Death, to a land whose gold mocks us not, and where everyone's "claim" is good, if he be found worthy to pass through the Golden Gate. Marshall, too, died a poor man, August 8th, 1885, having lived on a pension from the State of California, which also has seen fit to honour his memory, as the discoverer of gold, by erecting a monument to him at Coloma, the scene of the most exciting events in his life. The names of these two men, however, will endure in the thrilling histories of 1848 and 1849, as long as time lasts - for all unconsciously they set the civilised world in motion, gave new impulse to armies of men, spread sails on the ocean, filled coffers with yellow gold, and added new chapters to the graphic history of San Francisco and many another city. When the tidings of the discovery of gold reached the outside world thousands on thousands set their faces towards the El Dorado of the Pacific slopes. There were many new Jasons. The Golden Fleece of the sunny West was beckoning them on. New Argos were fitted out for the new Colchis. The Argonauts of 1849 were willing to brave all dangers. It is Joaquin Miller who sings -

> "Full were they
> Of great endeavour. Brave and true
> As stern Crusader clad in steel,
> They died afield as it was fit -
> Made strong with hope, they dared to do
> Achievement that a host to-day

Would stagger at, stand back and reel,
Defeated at the thought of it."

There were three ways of reaching the gold fields. Men could travel across the plains in the traditional emigrant wagon. It was a weary, lonely journey, life was endangered among hostile Indians, and happy were those who at last were strong enough to toil in the mines. Alas, too many fell by the way and left their bones to bleach in arid regions. It is the experience of life. We have our object of desire. We often come short of it. Ere we reach the goal we perish and the coveted prize is forever lost. Not so is it to him who seeks the Gold of New Jerusalem. The Gold of that land is good, and all who will can find it and enjoy it.

Another way was by the Isthmus of Panama, and then up the coast in such a ship as one could find. It was the least toilsome journey and the shortest, but still attended with hardships. Many fell a prey to wasting fevers which burn out one's life, and so never reached the destined port of San Francisco, through which they would pass to the gold fields.

The longest way was around Cape Horn. Still there were those who took it, even if months, five or six, it might be, were consumed in the journey. The gold they sought would compensate them at last. These too had to encounter storms, face probable shipwreck or contend with grim death. Many who sold all to equip themselves, who turned away from home and kindred, for a time they thought, to enrich themselves, who would surely return to their loved ones with untold treasure, never fulfilled their desire. Some perished in the voyage, others died in San Francisco, and were laid to rest till the final day in her cemeteries by the heaving ocean. Such as reached the mines did not always gain the gold they coveted. There were those who were fortunate, who made a success of life, who realised their day dreams; and some of these returned to the old home, to the waiting parents, to the longing wife and children. Some with their gold settled in San Francisco and sent for their kindred. And what happy meetings were those in the years of gold mining, when ships coming from many lands, from American and foreign ports, brought to the city through the Golden Gate the beloved ones whose dear faces had ever been an inspiration to the toilers in darkest hours! Methinks the meetings of loved ones parted here, on the shores of the crystal sea, will compensate for all life's labours and trials. Yes, if we only have the true treasures, the true gold of the Golden City.

In those days of 1848 and 1849 and during 1850 and 1851, San Francisco - on which we are now looking, the stately, comely city of to-day, was a city of tents in a large measure. Ships were pouring out their passengers at the Long Wharf. They would tent for a time on the shore, then hurry off to the mines. In those days you could meet in the streets men of various nationalities. Here were gold seekers from New England and old England, from our own Southland and the sunny land of France and Italy, from Germany and Sweden and Norway, from Canada and other British possessions, from China and Japan. And it was gold which brought them all here, the statesman and the soldier, the labouring man and the child of fortune, sons of adversity and sons of prosperity, rich and poor, lawyers, doctors, merchants, sailors, scholars, unlettered, - all are here for gold. Such is the San Francisco of those early days. It is a romance of reality, of the Golden West!

CHAPTER IV

THE STORY OF GOLDEN GATE PARK AND THE CEMETERIES

St. Andrew's Brotherhood - Patras - The Cross at Megara and the Golden Gate - Portsmouth Square and its Life - Other City Squares and Parks - Golden Gate Park, its Beauty, Objects and Places of Interest - Prayer Book Cross - Chance Visitors - Logan the Guide - First View of the Pacific Ocean - "Thy Way is in the Sea" - The Cemeteries of San Francisco - World-wide Sentiment - Group Around Lone Mountain - Story of the Graves - Earth's Ministries - Lesson of the Heavens.

When my companion Ashton and I landed at the Market Street Ferry House, an imposing structure of two stories, with a wide hall on the second floor and offices and bureaus of information on either side, our newfound friend, Mr. Young, bade us a "Good-by" with a hearty handshake, hoping he might meet us again. Before leaving us, however, he introduced us to a young man a member of the Brotherhood of St. Andrew, who took us to the temporary office of the Society in the Ferry House, and gave us necessary directions about the street cars, hotels and churches. We were in a strange city on the western shore of the Continent, yet, we felt at home at once through the cordial greeting of the Brotherhood. The St. Andrew's Cross, which our young guide wore on his coat, was indeed a friendly token. It spoke volumes to the heart; and I was carried back in memory to that early morning, when, having sailed over Ionian Seas, our good ship cast anchor in the Bay of Patras, and my feet pressed the soil which had been consecrated by the blood of the Saint, whose cross was now a token of good will and welcome at the ends of the earth. I could not but recall besides a memorable incident in connection with the Saint Andrew's Cross. We had passed the Isthmus of Corinth, and our train halted for a space at Megara, a town of six or seven thousand people, where is the bluest blood in all Greece; and as I alighted from my coach on the Athens and Peloponnesus Railway, I saw, some twenty rods away, a Greek Papa or Priest, who made a splendid figure. An impulse came over me to speak to him, and I knew there was one sign which he would recognise and understand. It was the Saint Andrew's Cross, which I made by crossing my arms. He immediately came to me and we conversed briefly as the time would permit, in the old language of Homer and Plato, which all patriotic Greeks love. He asked me if I was a Papa, and was pleased when I said, "Yes." I introduced him to my companions in the coach, and he greeted them warmly; and as the train began to move on we bade each other farewell. We may never meet again, but the Cross of Saint Andrew was a bond between us, and we felt that we were brethren in one Lord, Saint Andrew's Divine Master and ours. So the sight of that Cross there by the Pacific, with all its history of faith and love and martyrdom, caused our hearts to beat in unison with our brethren by the Golden Gate. I thought then it would be a special advantage to strangers in strange cities, if in some way the Brotherhood could serve as a Bureau of Information to travellers, who understand the meaning of the Cross. It would not be a matter of large expense after all if Chapters in large centres would extend greeting to men and women who are journeying hither and thither and who often stand in need of just such services as the Brotherhood could give. In a few hours after our arrival we were ready for the opening service of the General Convention, in Trinity Church, on Gough street at the corner of Bush street.

At intervals when duty would permit we made a study of San Francisco and its life, rich in scene and incident, and most instructive as well as attractive. Some of the noticeable features of the city are its parks and squares. In the northern part or section, Washington and Lobos Squares greet you, while Pioneer Park adorns Telegraph Hill, and Portsmouth Square or the Plaza is just east of the famous Chinese restaurant and close by police headquarters. This last was famous in the early days as the centre of Yerba Buena, and here the American flag was raised for the first time when our marines under Commodore Montgomery took possession of the town. Indeed some of the most exciting scenes in the early history of San Francisco were witnessed in this locality. Volumes might be written about its Spanish and Mexican families, its adobe buildings, its gambling places, its haunts of vice, its public assemblies, its crowds of men from all lands, its social and civic histories.

But all this is of the past, and it seems like a dream of by-gone days. When I visited it on two occasions, in company with friends, it was a quiet place enough; and the casual observer could never have thought or realised that around this romantic spot fortunes made by hard toil of weary months and years had been lost in a few short hours in the saloon and gambling places for which the vicinity was noted, that the worst passions of the human heart had been exhibited here, and that betimes amid the laughter of the merry throng in midnight revelry and above the strains of the "harp and viol" one could have heard the voices of blasphemy and the sharp, loud reports of pistols in the hands of careless characters, whose deadly bullets had sent many a poor unfortunate wayfarer or unwary miner from the gold fields to his long home.

If, in your saunterings, you go through the central part of the city you will find Lafayette Square, Alta Plaza, Hamilton Square, Columbia Square, and Franklin and Jackson Parks, at varying distances from each other and affording variety to the tourist. In the south section you will see Buena Vista Park and Garfield Square, while to the west you have Hill Park and Golden Gate Park. The Golden Gate Park is now famous the world over and vies in beauty and splendour with Central Park in New York, nay, in some respects surpasses this, in that it has a magnificent frontage on the Pacific ocean, a long coast view and a wide range of sea with the Farallone Islands, about twenty miles off in the foreground of the picture, and visible on a clear day always, and most enchanting in the sunset hour as we gazed on them. The Golden Gate Park dates back only to the year 1870, when the California Legislature passed an act providing for the improvement of public parks in San Francisco. At that time this lonely spot, now so like a dream of fairy land, was but a waste, a wide stretch of sand dunes among which the winds of the ocean played hide and seek. Its entrances, with a wide avenue in the foreground running north and south, are some five miles from the Market Street

Ferry. The afternoon that my friend Ashton and I visited it was clear and balmy. Just as we were entering the park carriage I was greeted by a young friend from the East, whom I had not seen for years; and then, more than three thousand miles away from home, I realised how small our planet is after all. As we rode along the flowery avenues with green lawns stretching out on either hand and losing themselves in groups of stately trees and hedges of shrubs and Monterey Cypress we were filled with delight. We could see the birds, native and foreign, flying from branch to branch of trees which grew within their gigantic cages, and occasionally we heard the notes of some songster. Yonder, too, we saw deer browsing, and elk and antelope. There also were the buffalo and the grizzly bear; and apparently all forgot that, shut in as they were in wide enclosures, they were in captivity. We could not fail to observe the bright flower-beds on every hand, the pleasant groves, the shady walks, the grottoes of wild design, the woodland retreats, the sylvan bowers. The park, we were told by our communicative driver, John Carter, comprises ten hundred and forty acres of ground. He also pointed out various places and objects of interest. The Museum, by the wayside, in its Egyptian architecture, is like one of the old temples of the Pharaohs on the banks of the Nile.

You are carried into the realm of immortal song when you gaze on the busts of Goethe and Schiller, and your patriotism is stirred afresh as you behold the monument of Francis Scott Key, author of the Star-Spangled Banner. The Muses also have their abode here on the colonnaded Music Stand or Pavilion erected by Claus Spreckles at a cost of $80,000. Another interesting feature is the Japanese Tea Garden.

Then there is the well equipped Observatory on Strawberry Hill from which you can look far out to sea, and where star-gazers can study celestial scenery as the Heavens declare God's glory. Seven lakelets give charm to the landscape, but the eye is never weary in looking on Stone Lake, a mile and a quarter in circuit, beautiful with its clear waters, its shelving shores, its bays and miniature headlands, while on its calm bosom, ducks of rich plumage and Australian swans are disporting themselves.

That, however, which attracted our attention most of all was the great grey stone cross on the crest of the highest point of the Golden Gate Park. This, chiseled after the fashion of the old crosses of Iona and linked with the name of St. Columba, is the monument erected by the late George W. Childs, of Philadelphia, Pa., to commemorate the first use of the Book of Common Prayer on the Pacific coast, when, in 1579, under Admiral Drake, Chaplain Fletcher read Prayers in this vicinity, either in San Francisco Bay, or a little further north in what is called Drake's Bay. But more of this anon. As we walked from the carriage road, beneath some spreading trees, to get a nearer view of the Prayer Book Cross, numerous partridges were moving about, without fear, in our pathway; and had we been minded to frighten them or do them harm we would have been restrained by yonder symbol of our redemption, which teaches us ever to be tender and humane towards bird and beast and all others of God's helpless creatures. The Prayer Book Cross is seen from afar. It looks down on the city with its innumerable homes, on the cemeteries within its shadow, on the Presidio with its tents and munitions of war, on the Golden Gate and on the waters of the Pacific, and it brings a blessing to all with its message of love and peace. It is a guide too, to the sailor coming over the seas from distant lands. As he strains his eyes to catch a glimpse of the coast the Cross stands out in bold relief against the eastern sky, and it tells him that he will find a hospitable welcome and safe harbourage within the Golden Gate. So it is dear to him after his voyage over stormy seas as was of old

"Sunium's marbled steep"

to the Greek sailor nearing home.

Near Stone Lake we met the head commissioner of the Park who saluted us with all the easy grace of the Californian; and on the way we had the opportunity of receiving a Scotch gentleman and his wife into our carriage; and, later, a clergyman who had been wandering about in the midst of sylvan scenes, rode with us to the entrance of the Park, where we bade our new found friends good-bye, each to go his own way, at eventide.

The third day after our arrival in San Francisco I had a longing to gaze on the Pacific ocean which I had never seen. There were no laurels for us to win, such as Balboa justly deserved when he discovered the Pacific and first beheld its wide waters in the year 1513; but it was a natural desire to look on its broad expanse and to stand on its shores, along which bold navigators had sailed since the days of Cabrillo and Drake. Taking a line of cars running out to the Presidio, Ashton and I walked the rest of the way. A young man named Logan, a cousin of the famous General Logan, who was in the service of the government as a mail carrier, but off duty that afternoon, volunteered most courteously to be our guide. He accompanied us for more than a mile and a half of the distance beyond the Presidio, but then had to return to meet an engagement. We went forward climbing the steep hills and finally found that we were standing on the heights above the immense ocean, in the grounds of the Government Reservation. It was a solemn moment when we for the first time beheld the Pacific, and we were greatly impressed. There the mighty waters, across which the ships sail to China and Japan and the Sandwich Islands and the Philippine Archipelago and the South Seas, lay before our eyes. The darkness of the night was coming on, but the sky far off across the waters, away beyond the Farallone Islands, was tinged with red and gold, the fading glories of the dying day. We could see in the glow of evening the heaving of the sea and the motion of its comparatively calm surface, in that twilight hour.

Gathering clouds hung over the horizon and formed the shadows in the picture. Every picture has light and shade. It is a portrait of life. We stood silently for a time drinking in all the beauty of the scene, well nigh entranced, awed, thrilled betimes; and at last in order to give fitting expression to the thoughts within our hearts, I suggested that we should hold a brief service in recognition of His power who holds the seas in the hollow of His hands, Who had guided our feet in safe paths and byways of the world, often over its troublesome waves. Ashton said an appropriate Collect from the dear old Prayer Book of so many tender and far off memories, while I expressed my feelings in the grand words of the Psalm - "Thy way is in the sea, and Thy paths in the great waters, and Thy footsteps are not known." We felt God's presence in that hushed hour, we saw in vision the divine Christ walking over the waters to us!

In our wanderings about the city the sleeping places of the dead naturally attracted our attention; and where, especially, on Sunday afternoons, the living congregate to mourn over their loved ones, to scatter flowers on their graves, or to while away an hour amid scenes which have a melancholy interest and tend to sobriety and remind one of another land where there is no death for those who pass through the Golden Gate of eternity. Cemeteries have always attracted the living to their solemn precincts at stated times, anniversaries and fiestas. It is so in all lands, among all peoples no matter what their creed, and in all ages. Jew and Gentile alike, Mohammedan and Christian, by visiting tomb or grassy mound with some token of their affection, the prayer uttered, the tear shed, the blossoms laid on sacred soil, after this manner cherish the memories of the departed. And it is well! Scenes which the traveller may witness in the Campo Santo of Genoa or in the Koimeteria of Athens, on Sundays, in the Mezaristans of Skutari on the Bosphorus and Eyub on the Golden Horn, on Friday afternoons, and in the Kibroth of old Tiberias by the Sea of Galilee or outside of the walls of Jerusalem, on Saturday or in the Cimenterios of Mexico City on fiestas, all testify to the universality of the deep and tender feelings of reverence and affection which animate the human heart and make all men as one in thought and sentiment as they stand on time's shores and follow the receding forms of their kindred and friends with wishful eyes bedimmed with tears across the Dark River!

While there is a Burial Place for the soldiers who die for their country or in their country's cause, on the grounds of the Presidio, the principal cemeteries of San Francisco seem to cluster around Lone Mountain in the northwestern part of the city and south of the Military

Reservation. These are Laurel Hill, Calvary, Masonic and Odd Fellows. The Jews have their special burying ground between Eighteenth and Twentieth streets, and the old Mission cemetery where some of the early Indian converts and Franciscan Fathers sleep their last sleep, is close by the Mission Dolores, on the south side.

The group around Lone Mountain is dominated by a conspicuous cross on the hill top, which, as a sentinel looks down with a benison on the resting places of the dead, and, in heat and cold, in storm and sunshine, seems to speak to the heart about Him "Who died, and was buried, and rose again for us." To this picturesque spot too the Chinese have been attracted, and they bury their departed west of Laurel Hill, with all the rites peculiar to the followers of Confucius.

But what thrilling histories of men from many lands are entombed in all these tens of thousands of graves, what fond hopes are buried here, what withered blossoms of life mingle with this consecrated soil by the waters of the Pacific! Many a one who sought the Golden West in pursuit of fortune found all too soon his goal here with unfulfilled desire, while anxious friends and relatives beyond the seas and the mountains or on the other side of the continent awaited his home coming for years in vain. Here, indeed, are no rolls of papyrus, no hieroglyphics, as in Egyptian tombs, to tell us the story of the past, but it is written in the experiences of the gold seekers, it is interwoven with the life of the city, now the mistress of the great ocean which laves her feet, and it is burned into the memories of many living witnesses.

If yonder grave could tell its tale it would speak to you

of a misspent life which might have been a blessing - of midnight revels and mad excesses and Circe's feasts, the ruin of soul and body. And this grave could talk to you about one who, far away from home and kindred, had pined and wasted away in his loneliness, and had died of homesickness. But while you are touched with the pathetic recital, that grave near by reads you a lesson of patience, of heroism, of faith, of purity of soul and body preserved in the midst of fiery temptations, even while strong men were yielding themselves up to "fleshly lusts which war against the soul."

The shrubs and trees and flowers on which you gaze, and which are green and blossom the year round, now beautify all and mother earth softens with her ministries the severities of the past, and sunlit skies bend over the dead, as of old in many lands, and star-bedecked heavens tell still to the living, as once to those whose bodies mouldered here, the story of the life beyond, where glory and riches and honour are the heritage of the faithful!

CHAPTER V

THEN AND NOW,
OR EIGHTEEN HUNDRED FORTY-NINE AND NINETEEN HUNDRED AND ONE

Triangular Section of San Francisco - Clay Banks, Mud and Rats in 1849 - Streets at That Time - Desperate Characters - Gambling Houses - Thirst for Gold - Saloons and Sirens - The Bella Union - The Leaven of the Church - Robbers' Dens and Justice in Mining Camps - The Vigilance Committee and What It Did - San Francisco Well Governed Now - Highway Robbers and the Courts - Chief of Police Wittman and His Men - A Visit to Police Headquarters - The Cells - A Murderer - A Chinese Woman in Tears - A Hardened Offender.

The traveller to the City of the Golden Gate, as he approaches it, having crossed the great bay from Oakland, notices that the hundreds of streets which greet his gaze run from east to west, and cross each other at right angles, except a triangular section of this metropolis of the west. This part of the city may be compared to a great wedge with the broad end on the bay. It begins at the Market Street Ferry house and runs south as far as South Street at the lower end of China Basin. This triangle is bounded on the north by Market Street, which follows a line west by southwest, and on the south by Channel and Ridley Streets, the latter crossing Market Street at the sharp end of the wedge-shaped section. The portion of the city within the triangle embraces in its water-front the Mission, Howard, Folsom, Stewart, Spear, Fremont, and Merrimac Piers, together with Mail and Hay Docks. Here you may see steamships and sailing vessels from all parts of the world moored at their piers, while others are riding at anchor a little way out from the land. The whole scene is at once picturesque and animated and suggests great activity. We must remember, however, that where now are these massive piers with their richly laden ships and noble argosies, as far back only as 1849 there were no stable docks, no properly constructed wharfs, no convenient landing places. Here only were clay banks, which gave no promise of the great future with its commercial grandeur, and everything was insecure and unsatisfactory, especially in rainy weather, which began in November and continued with more or less interruption until April. The new comer, not cautious to secure a sure footing would sometimes sink deep in the soft mud or even disappear in the spongy earth. With the ships too came not only the gold-seekers from many lands, but rats also as if they had a right and title to the rising city. These swarmed along the primitive wharfs, and at times they would invade the houses and tents of the people and go up on their beds or find a lodging-place in vessels and cup-boards. Some of these rodents which followed in the wake of the new civilisation were from China and Japan, while others, gray and black, came in ships from Europe and from American cities on the Atlantic seaboard. Even wells had to be closed except at the time of the drawing of water, in order to keep out these pests which made the life of many a householder well nigh intolerable.

The streets were few in number then, not more than fifteen or twenty, as the town, at the time of which we are speaking, had only a population of about five thousand people. As San Francisco grew, however, under the impetus which the discovery of gold gave to it, the streets were naturally multiplied; and, to over come the mire in wet weather and also the sand of the dry season, which made it difficult for pedestrians to walk hither and thither or for vehicles to move to and fro, they were planked in due time. Wooden sewers were also constructed on each side of the street to carry off the surface water. A plank road besides ran out to Mission Dolores, the vicinity of which was a great resort on Sundays, especially in the days when "bull fighting" was a pastime and the old Spanish and Mexican elements of the population had not been eliminated or had not lost their prestige.

As one went to and fro then and encountered men of all nationalities, it was not an uncommon thing to meet many who had the look of desperadoes, whose upper garment was a flannel shirt, while revolvers looked threateningly out of their belts at the passerby. All this of course, was changed after a time, when the days of reform came, as they always come when the need arises. There is an element in human society which acts as a corrective, and wrong is finally dethroned, and right displays her power with a divine force and a vivid sweep as a shaft of lightning from the sky. We need never despair about the triumph of the good. It is a noble sentiment which Bryant utters in "The Battle Field:"

> "Truth crushed to earth shall rise again:
> The eternal years of God are hers;
> But Error, wounded, writhes in pain,

And dies among his worshippers."

And never was there a community or a city where Truth asserted her sway more potently in the midst of evil than in San Francisco in the trying days of her youth. With the rush from all lands to California for the coveted gold came the lawless and the bloodthirsty. Men in the gambling houses would sometimes quarrel over the results of the game or over some "love affair." Fair Helen and unprincipled, gay, thoughtless Paris were here by the Golden Gate. The old story is constantly repeating itself since the Homeric days. Duels were fought betimes as a consequence, and the issue for one or both of the combatants was generally fatal. Gambling in those days was, from a worldly stand-point, the most profitable business, that is for the professional player or the saloon-keeper. Indeed it was looked upon as quite respectable. It has a strange fascination at all times for a certain class, with whom it becomes a passion as much as love for the wine-cup, and one must be well grounded in principle to resist its influences. Many once noble souls who had been tenderly brought up were led astray. Away from home and its restraining associations, gambling, drinking, and other sins and vices became their ruin. In calm moments when alone or under some momentary impulse of goodness there would rise before them the vision of God-fearing parents - of open Bibles - of hallowed Sundays; but the thirst for gold could not be quenched, the mad race must be run, and to the bitter end, dishonour, death, the grave! Shelley, if he had stood in the midst of the gamblers, staking all, even their souls, for gold, in those California days of wild revelry, could not have expressed himself more appositely than in his graphic and truthful lines, in Queen Mab:

> "Commerce has set the mark of selfishness;
> The signet of its all-enslaving power
> Upon a shining ore, and called it gold:
> Before whose image bow the vulgar great,
> The vainly rich, the miserable proud,
> The mob of peasants, nobles, priests, and kings,
> And with blind feelings reverence the power
> That grinds them to the dust of misery.
> But in the temple of their hireling hearts
> Gold is a living god, and rules in scorn
> All earthly things but virtue."

The saloons fifty years ago were the centres of attraction for the over-wrought miner, the aimless wanderer, the creature of impulse, the child of passion. They were decorated with an eye to brilliant colours, to gorgeous effect, to all that appeals to the sensuous element in our nature. They were the best built and most richly furnished houses in the San Francisco of that period. The walls were adorned with costly paintings, and the furniture was in keeping with this lavish outlay. In each gambling house was a band of music, and a skillful player received some $30 per night for his services. Painted women were the presiding geniuses at the wheels of fortune and these modern Circes or Sirens played the piano and the harp with all the passion of their art to drown men's cares and make them forget duty and principle and honour. The tables of the players of the games were piled high with yellow gold to serve as a tempting bait. The games were chiefly what are called in the nomenclature of the gambling fraternity. Rouge-et-noir, Monte-faro, and Roulette. The men who lost, whatever their feelings might be, and they were often bitter, as a rule disguised their sore disappointment. They would try their luck again, but this only led them deeper in the mire. Many an one lost a princely fortune in a night. The gambling houses were located chiefly around the Plaza or Portsmouth Square, of which we have already spoken. They were filled, as a general thing, all night, with an eager throng, especially on Sunday. Indeed everything then had its full course on Sunday. There were various sports; drinking and gambling ran riot. Blasphemous words filled the air. Men swore without the least thought. But profanity is not alone restricted to a frontier or border community, where laws and a sense of propriety are wanting. One may hear it in old and civilised towns, as he walks the streets, and sometimes from the lips of boys. In these saloons people of all ages congregated from youth up to hoary hairs. Here were the Indian and the Negro, the American and the Mexican, the Spaniard and the Frenchman, the Italian, the Dutchman and the German, the Dane and the Russian, the English, the Irish and the Scotchman, the Chinaman and the Japanese. One of the most noted of the saloons was the Bella Union, a Monte Carlo in itself. Woe betide the miner from the mountains with gold who entered it. Here was a richly appointed bar to tempt the desire for drink, while costly mirrors were arranged in such wise as to reflect the scenes of revelry, and pictures that were worth large sums of money hung on the walls. The silverware too would have done credit to a royal board. Both the tables and the bar were well patronised at all times.

Naturally with such elements of society, with the mad thirst for gold, with the loose morality which prevailed to a large extent, there would be great lawlessness. It must be borne in mind however that the Christian Church was at work in those perilous times, which live only in memory now, and was gradually leavening the whole lump. There were devout men and true women in early San Francisco, who, in the midst of "a crooked generation," kept themselves pure and "unspotted from the world." And is it not true that men can hold fast their crown, that no man take it from them, if only they will make use of the grace of God? God has His faithful witnesses in every place, in every age, no matter how corrupt. There are the "seven thousand" who do not bow the kneel to Baal, there are the faithful "few names" even in Sardis who do not defile their garments with the world. San Francisco had them in those days of special temptation, brave and noble souls who could say with Sir Galahad:

> "My strength is as the strength of ten,
> Because my heart is pure."

In this strength they rose up and purged the place, even though as difficult as a labour of Hercules. The men of the Vigilance Committee will ever live in song and story. Even up in the mountains in the gold mines of El Dorado county and elsewhere the spirit of the men of San Francisco was at work in the camps. Robbers were there, bold characters, dark-browed men, who would not hesitate to steal, and kill, if need be, in their nefarious work. The miners had their perils to encounter in these bandits. The robbers had their dens in the mountains in lonely places, beside a trail sometimes, and in the depths of the forests. The dens had generally two rooms on the ground floor and a loft which was reached by a ladder. If a belated miner sought shelter or food here he was given a lodging in the loft. If he drank with his "host" it would most likely be some liquor that was drugged, and in his heavy sleep he was sure to be robbed. In the morning he had no redress, and he might consider himself fortunate if he escaped with his life. Sometimes however the robber was brought to quick justice by the miners. Robbery was not countenanced in the camps. If one should steal, his fellows would rise up, try him in a hastily convened court, and condemn him to death, and hang him on the nearest tree. It was a rule that the body should be exposed for twenty-four hours as a warning to others. All this may seem harsh, but under the circumstances it was the only way in which justice could be dealt out to offenders. The camps were in consequence orderly and safe. We must not think, because the Vigilance Committees of the mining camps and of the city took the administration of law into their own hands that therefore they were lawless and that their rule was that of the mob. No, this was the only way in which peaceable citizens could be protected from the violence and crimes perpetrated by the turbulent and disorderly and vicious elements of society. In the years 1851 and 1852 there was great lawlessness in San Francisco. Bad men, who had served terms in prisons for their misdeeds, and men who wished to disorganise society, who had the spirit of anarchy in their breasts, organised themselves into bands for the purpose of stealing and killing, and good citizens stood in mortal fear of them. Buildings were burned at pleasure, houses were broken open and robberies committed, and even murder was resorted to when the wrongdoers found it necessary in the accomplishment of their hellish purposes. The officials of the city were careless in punishing offenders, indeed they were powerless to do so, and the lawbreakers knew this. It is said that over a hundred persons were murdered during the period of six months; and the blood of these victims cried to Heaven for vengeance. To assert the majesty of law and to punish criminals a large number of the best citizens, who grieved over the evils which prevailed, organised themselves into the famous Vigilance Committee. The seal which they adopted showed their worthy purpose. In the centre was the figure of a human eye to denote watchfulness. Above the eye was the word, Committee, - beneath, Vigilance; then the name, San Francisco. Around the edge of the seal ran the legends: "Fiat Justitia Ruat Coelum. No creed; no party; no sectional issues." While not constituted exactly like the Court of Areopagus, yet the Vigilance Committee of San Francisco did for a time exercise authority over life and death like the Athenian judges on Mars' Hill. The shaft of lightning first fell on an ex-convict who was caught stealing. Eighty members of the Committee tried and convicted him, and on the same night he was hanged in Portsmouth Square in view of the saloons. A thrill ran through the whole community, and when, the next morning, the people read the names of the prominent citizens who served on the Committee, their action made a deep and salutary impression. The Vigilance Committee prosecuted its work till the city was purged of its evils, and it exercised from time to time its authority until the year 1856. As a result of its firmness, its promptness in punishing criminals, and its high-minded aims, the land had rest for twenty years. A weak administration of justice is an encouragement to wrong doing. Municipal and state officials can best serve their city and country by dealing quick and severe blows at lawlessness; but to be effective they must be men of integrity, above reproach, and withal just. To-day San Francisco is one of the most orderly and best governed cities in the United States. During my rambles through its streets I went to and fro at all hours without being molested. I never met a drunken man or a disorderly person. The city feels the effect of the Committee's good work even to this latest hour. It serves as an example. Justice is dealt out speedily to offenders. There are few if any technical delays of the law and the criminal rarely escapes without punishment. Some examples have occurred recently which show that the judges of the superior courts are alive to their duty and that they can perform it when the occasion arises. A man named John H. Wood, a former soldier, was convicted of highway robbery, and he was speedily sentenced to imprisonment for life in Folsom Penitentiary. Judge Cook who passed sentence on him took the position that a man who used a deadly weapon in the commission of his crime should receive the full penalty of the law. A man who holds a pistol to shoot will take life, therefore he ought to have a life sentence. Wood, who belongs to a wealthy family in Texas, has a checkered history. He served as a soldier for a time in the Philippine Islands. Here he deserted his post and committed highway robbery. He was tried by court martial for larceny and convicted. Then he was brought to San Francisco and put in the military prison on the Island of Alcatraz. He was finally discharged from the army in disgrace. A few months ago he tried to rob a showcase man and held a revolver at his head while he seized a watch and chain. He was immediately arrested by three officers, and a month after he was sentenced for life. As showing the depravity of the man he said after receiving sentence: "That is an awful dose, and I haven't had my breakfast yet." Possibly in prison he will reflect upon his evil life, and be softened, and repent. He might have been a good citizen, worthy of his country; but he hardened his heart and sank deeper and deeper in his degradation. Oh, the hardening of the heart! It was Pharaoh's sin. It is the sin of many an one now.

Another highway robber, Edward Davis, was sentenced at the same time with Wood to serve in the

State Penitentiary for thirty-three years. He also pointed a pistol to the head of his victim. But thirty-three years! He will probably die in prison. It is a life thrown away, one of God's best gifts. But if stern justice be meted out here in this world, what must the unrepenting sinner, who has trampled the divine law under foot, expect in the world to come? San Francisco teaches a lesson which reaches farther than an earthly tribunal. The judge on his bench is an image of the Judge who weighs human life in His balances.

There is of course crime in San Francisco as in all other cities. Indeed crime is universal, whether in the Orient or the Occident. The Chief of Police Wittman accounts for highway robbery, to the extent in which it prevails, from the fact that San Francisco is a garrison city. Here are numerous recruits and discharged soldiers, and, as a seaport, it draws to itself the scum and offscourings of all nations, Hindoos, Chinese, Malays, and all other kinds of people.

The police force is hardly adequate to patrol the entire city. It consists only of 589 men all told, and they are fine, manly looking guardians of the law, always ready to do their duty, always courteous to strangers, answering all questions intelligently. It is claimed, moreover, that the criminal element of the country drifts to San Francisco in the winter on account of the climate and also through the attractions of the racetrack. The police also find that the places where poker-games are played are a rendezvous for criminals. In 1887 and 1888 there was an outbreak of highway robbery, but the grand jury acted promptly in the matter and the courts soon suppressed it. Property and life therefore are jealously guarded in the City of the Golden Gate, and bad characters who go thither to prey on the public soon get their deserts. In this respect then San Francisco is a desirable place in which to live.

One evening in company with a party of friends, Rev. Dr. Ashton of Clean, N.Y., Rev. Dr. Reynold Marvin Kirby of Potsdam, N.Y., Rev. Clarence Ernest Ball of Alexandria, Va., Rev. Henry Sidney Foster of Green Bay, Wis., the Rev. William Barnaby Thorne of Marinette, Wis., and Doctor Robert J. Gibson, surgeon in the United States Army, stationed at San Francisco, I visited the police headquarters, situated on the east side of Portsmouth Square. This is a large building of several stories with numerous offices. The chief in his office on the main floor, on the right hand of the entrance, received us courteously and assigned to us a detective according to an arrangement previously made with Ashton. In the office were portraits of police commissioners and the chiefs and others who had been connected with the department for many years. Entering an elevator we were soon on the topmost floor where were the cells in which prisoners just arrested and waiting for trial were confined. The doors of the cells, all of iron, were opened or closed by moving a lever. It was now about 9:30 P.M., and officers were bringing in such persons as had been arrested for theft, for assault and battery, for drunkenness and other kinds of evil doing. Towards daybreak the cells are pretty well filled, but now they were nearly empty. How true His words who knows what is in man. "Men love darkness rather than light because their deeds are evil!"

One young man who had killed another in a quarrel was pointed out to us. The woman who loved him and who expected to be his wife, and still had faith in him, was at his side, with her sister, conversing with him between her sobs, in a low earnest tone. He seemed greatly agitated. A detective stood a little way off from the trio. The evidence was strong against the murderer, and an officer said to us that there was no chance for him to escape from the penalty of the law. In a cell was a young Chinese woman, just brought in, possibly for disorderly conduct. She could not have been more than fifteen or sixteen years old. She was pretty and refined in appearance and handsomely dressed, and she wept as if her heart would break. Not yet hardened by sin, and probably imprisoned for the first time, she felt the shame and degradation of her lot. I could not but feel pity for her, and expressed sorrow for her, though she may not have understood my words. At least she could interpret the signs of sympathy in voice and expression. These are a universal language. Maybe she was more sinned against than sinning, - and that Divine One Who reads all hearts and knows the temptations and snares which beset unwary feet, would say to her - "Go, and sin no more!"

In another cell was an old offender who had a face furrowed with sin. As we looked at her I could see that she regarded our presence as an intrusion. I recalled Dr. Watt's lines:

> "Sinners who grow old in sin
> Are hardened in their crimes."

Yet there is an awakening of the conscience at last, and even a prison house with its corrections may be a door of escape from that other prison of the sinful soul from which no one can go forth, be he culprit or juror, counsellor or judge, until his pardon is pronounced by Him who can forgive sins.

CHAPTER VI

FROM STREET NOMENCLATURE
TO A CANNON

The Streets of the City - Numbers and Names - Example of Athens - Names of Men - Names of States and Countries - American Spirit - Flowers and Trees - Market Street - Pleasantries - Mansions of California Avenue - Grand Reception - Art in California - Cost of Living in 1849 - Hotels and Private Houses now - Restaurants - New City Hall - Monumental Group - Scenes and Representations - History of a Cannon - Chance Meeting with General Shafter - Mission of the Republic.

The streets of the city! They are an important feature, and the traveller naturally observes their direction and studies their character. In the description of New Jerusalem, St. John noted the fact that its street was "pure gold." The streets of earthly cities cannot vie with the celestial, though the gold of commerce may be found in their warehouses and mansions; but if men were as earnest in seeking after the treasures of Heaven as were the tens of thousands who flocked to the gold-fields of California in 1849, they would surely win the fortune which awaits them within the Golden Gate of the City on the banks of the Crystal River. San Francisco has her noted streets, just as the City of

Mexico has her San Francisco promenade, leading from the Alameda to the Plaza de Zocalo; or Rome her famous Corso, the old Via Flaminia, with its shops and its teeming life; or Athens her Hodos Hermou, with its old Byzantine church of Kapnikaraea; or Constantinople her Grande Rue de Pera, with its hotels and theatres and bazaars; or old Damascus, her "street that is called straight," Suk et-Tawileh, the street of the Long Bazaar, with its Oriental life and colouring; or Cairo her picturesque Muski, where you may find illustrations of scenes in the Arabian Nights, and gratify your senses with

> "Sabean odours from the spicy shore
> Of Araby the Blest."

The streets of the city by the Golden Gate have an interesting nomenclature, which well deserves one's study for what it teaches. Some streets in the triangular section of San Francisco, already spoken of, are numbered. These begin west of Fremont street and run up to Thirteenth, being bounded by Market street. Then the numbered streets take a turn to the left hand and go from Fourteenth to Twenty-Sixth, in the southwestern section of the city, and run due west. Numbers on the streets of any city are of course a convenience, but such a nomenclature has nothing else to commend it, and lacks imagination and sacrifices bits of history which may be interwoven with municipal life and show progress from small beginnings and perpetuate pioneers' names and benefactors' memories. Modern Athens in naming her streets has very wisely called them after some of the demigods, heroes, generals, statesmen, and poets of Greece; and grateful too for the work of Lord Byron in behalf of her independence, she has honoured him who in immortal song spurred on her sons to arise and cast off the Turkish yoke, with a name on one of her thoroughfares - Hodos Tou Buronos - which the traveller reads with emotion, even as he gazes also with admiration on the beautiful Pentelic monument reared to the memory of her benefactor, near the Arch of Hadrian, while Athenae is represented as crowning him with the victorious olive. With feelings and sentiments akin to this the sons of the Golden West have associated forever with the streets of their great city the names of men who either benefited California or take high rank in national life or are otherwise worthy of perpetual commemoration. Hence we have a Berkeley street, a Buchanan, a Castro, a Fillmore, a Franklin, a Fremont, a Grant, a Hancock, a Harrison, a Hawthorne, and a Humboldt street. Juniper street is a memorial of Father Junipero Serra, founder of Franciscan Missions. Kepler takes us up to the stars, which shine beautifully over the lofty Sierras, California's eternal rampart; while Lafayette speaks to us of friendship and chivalry, still alive in these matter of fact days. As you walk through the streets you see also the name of Kearney, not Dennis of "sand-lot" fame, but that of General S.W. Kearney, whose sword aided in placing the star of California in our Nation's Flag; you read too the name of the old Indian chief, Marin, and that of Montezuma takes you across the Rio Grande and back to the days of Mexican romance and barbaric splendour. Here also Montgomery is remembered, the patriotic commander of the Portsmouth, who gave orders to his marines to raise the Stars and Stripes, in place of Spanish ensigns and the Bear Flag, on the Plaza of Yerba Buena, old San Francisco, in 1846. We find also such well known names as Scott, Sherman and Stanford. We have too a St. Francis street and a St. Joaquin street; Sumner, Sutter, Tilden and Webster are remembered also.

Nearly all the states of the Union speak to us by these waters of the Pacific in the stones of the streets. All the original Thirteen except Georgia have been honoured. Possibly this will receive recognition in the future. It is to be noted, however, that the adjectives are omitted in the Carolinas and New Hampshire. New York is the exception together with Rhode Island. The other States which have given their names to streets are Alabama, Arkansas, California, the Dakotas without the qualifying adjective, Florida, Illinois, Indiana, Iowa, Kansas, Kentucky, Louisiana, Michigan, Minnesota, Missouri, Nebraska, Nevada, Tennessee, Utah, Vermont, Wisconsin and Wyoming. The natural inference from this is that San Francisco has drawn her population from all parts of the land; so that here you have representatives of our great country, north, south, east and west gathered together. While there are many who delight to call themselves Native Sons, yet their fathers have sprung from households in New England and in the South and in the Middle States and elsewhere and new peoples are steadily migrating to the Pacific slopes, notably to this Queen City by the Golden Gate. In my intercourse with San Franciscans, this or that worthy citizen would say, with no little pride, I was born in New York, Boston is my birthplace, I am a native of Albany, or Saratoga, or Philadelphia, or Baltimore, or Savannah or New Orleans. Sometimes one would say to me, I came from the East. What part? The answer would be at times, Chicago, or St. Louis, or Omaha, as the case might be. But one thing was very noticeable, that they were all loyal Americans. I think it may be truly said that the spirit of patriotism is even stronger in the Pacific States than at the East. You could see the Flag of the Union everywhere, and there was abundant evidence in the life and speech of the people of San Francisco and of California generally that they were an integral part of the Republic and as anxious to have it prosperous and great and united as the most ardent American in any other part of the land.

The cosmopolitan character of San Francisco is further indicated by the names of foreign countries and places which some of her streets bear. Here we note in our walks the names of Denmark and Japan, Honduras and Montenegro, Trinidad, Venezuela and Valencia, and also the Spanish town De Haro. Certain names also of cities tell us whence people have come to the City of the Golden Gate. We find an Albany, an Austin, and a Chattanooga street. There are also streets called Erie, Hartford, Vicksburg and York, San Jose and Santa Clara, while Fair Oaks speaks of one of the great battlefields of the Civil War. Some of the counties of the State have also fixed their names on the streets as Butte, El Dorado, Mariposa, Napa, Solano and Sonoma. The Potomac River has a name here also, while Sierra and Shasta represent the mountains. There are names of streets besides which take us among the trees and shrubs, such as the Cedar, the Locust, the Linden, the Oak, the Walnut, the Willow, the Ivy, the Laurel and the Myrtle. Of flowers there is a profusion in San Francisco. They bloom on every hand; and wherever there is a bit of ground or lawn in front of a house there you will see plants or flowers in blossom. Fuschias attain the height of ten feet in some places and are magnificent in the colour and beauty of their flowers. The heliotrope climbs up its support with eagerness and its blossoms vie in hue with the blue skies. You may also see the pink flowers of the Malva plant in abundance, the chaste mignonette and the Australian pea-vine. The latter is a favourite and clothes the bare walls of fence or house or trellis with a robe of beauty which queens might envy. Roses are rich and fragrant, white and pink chiefly, and delight the eye, no matter which way you turn. The Acacia grows here in San Francisco as if it were native to the soil; and the Monterey Cypress, green and beautiful, makes a handsome hedge, or, when given room and air, it attains to stately proportions. Here also you will find the Eucalyptus tree in its perfection, stately in form with its ivy-green foliage, and you look upon it with an admiring eye. California may be truly called a land of flowers as well as a land of fruits; and we err not in judgment when we say that close association with these beautiful products of the earth has a refining and an uplifting influence on the human heart. A man who has love for a flower is brought near to the Lord of the flowers, Who said as He walked over the meadows of Palestine - "Consider the lilies of the field, how they grow." So they have their sweet message of love and gentleness and peace for all, yes, these "stars of the earth," as the poet calls them. Such thoughts come to you as you gaze on the rich gardens of San Francisco and note their wealth of bright blossoms, brightening man's life and filling his soul with poetry and sentiment and longing for the beautiful and for the good.

As we walk through the city we note that it is rapidly extending itself towards the south and the slopes of the Pacific, and new homes are constantly appearing in its suburbs, even climbing up the hills to the west. Market street, broad and straight, is San Francisco's main artery of business activity, and the cable cars which run through it are so numerous that a person who undertakes to cross this great avenue, especially during the busy hours of the day, must be careful lest he be run over. It reminds one of Broadway, New York, in this respect. All streets of the city converge towards Market street. Crowds of people throng it, and this is true, particularly during Saturday night, when the labours of the week are ended and the populace seek recreation. There are many large and attractive buildings on this street, as for example "The Call Building," "The Chronicle Building," "The Palace Hotel," and the "Emporium." As you walk up and down studying life you note many things, and you see good nature depicted in the faces of the people whom you meet. They all look bright and intelligent. I think there is something in the surroundings and in the exhilarating atmosphere which promotes fellowship and good feeling. There is a keen sense of humour often manifest. Among many of the things which I saw was an illuminated sign, with the legend: "Your bosom friend." As I drew near it I discovered that it was over a shirt store. It was certainly most suggestive. The women, as you see them going hither and thither, are the picture of health and many of them can boast of real beauty. Here are few if any pale faces, sallow complexions, cadaverous cheeks. There are various types of nationality, but it may be said that there is a California or San Francisco type, which is the product of climate and environment. One is struck with the animation manifested in the faces and movements of the men and women. They are quick too in reaching conclusions and witty in observation. A young man in one of the railway offices asked this question: "What," said he to me, "is the difference in dress between a bishop and any other clergyman," I replied that some of the bishops wore aprons, and that this was the only real difference in daily attire - except some special mark on the coat or the shape of the hat. I hastened to add by way of pleasantry, that my friend Ashton, who was standing beside me, and I had not an apron as yet. "Well," he replied promptly, "you have gotten beyond that."

They take pleasure in telling a good story also. As Ashton and I were travelling one afternoon to San Rafael we were joined on the Saucelito ferry boat by a benevolent gentleman, named Ingram, who said he was a cousin of the Bishop of London. As we talked over various matters he finally said, "I will tell you a story. An Irishman landed in New York after a stormy voyage; and as he walked up Broadway he thought that he would go into the first place he saw, which looked like a Roman Catholic church, and there offer thanks for his safe journey. When he came to St. Paul's Chapel, with the statute of the Apostle in view, he went into it, and kneeling down he began to cross himself. The sexton seeing his demonstrations said to him, 'This is not a Roman church, this is a Protestant church.' But said he, 'It is a Catholic church. Don't you see the cross and the candles on the altar.' 'O no,' said the sexton in reply, 'It is a Protestant church.' 'No, no,' said the Irishman, 'you can't convince me that St. Paul turned Protestant when he came to America!'"

One is impressed with the air of prosperity and thrift on every hand. Many of the houses are artistic in construction and elegant in their furnishings. Some of them are stately mansions, notably the Stanford, Huntington, Hopkins and Crocker residences on California avenue, in its most conspicuous section. The homes of these California kings are adorned with costly works of art, choice paintings, and beautifully chiselled marbles. During the sessions of the General Convention the Crocker mansions on the north side of the avenue were the centre of attraction in the liberal hospitality dispensed there and the courtesies shown to many of the Bishops and other Clergy. On the evening of Wednesday, October the ninth, Bishop Nichols held a reception for the Bishops, other Clergy, the Lay

Deputies, and their friends, in the Hopkins' mansion, on the south side of California avenue. This is now used as an Art Institute, and it is admirably adapted to its purpose. The building was thronged all the evening by the members of the Convention and the representatives of San Francisco society. Five thousand people high in the councils of the Church and the Nation and in social walks were in attendance; and it was impossible to accommodate all who came. It is said that hundreds were turned away. The writer and his friends considered themselves fortunate to be able to thread their way through the crowd without being crushed or having their garments torn. It was the grandest function of a social character which ever took place on the Pacific coast. The costly paintings adorning chambers, galleries and reception rooms, the splendid specimens of statuary, the numerous pictures, the brilliant lights, the strains of joyous music, but above all the moving throng of handsome women beautifully arrayed, and the noble bearing of Bishop, Priest and layman, with the fine intellectual faces seen on all sides, made this reception a scene never to be forgotten. Who, in the days of forty-nine, would have dreamed that, a little over a half a century later, there would be such a magnificent gathering of intellect and beauty, - men and women with lofty aims and noted for their achievements in letters and art, and their prominence in Church and State, and excelling in virtuous deeds, on a hill which was then a barren waste of shifting sands?

While I am speaking of the reception in the Hopkins' Art Institute, I may note that Californians have a great love for art. Their own grand scenery of mountain and valley and ocean fosters the love for the beautiful; and to-day they can point with pride to the works of such men as Julian Rix, Charles Dickman, H.J. Bloomer, J.M. Gamble, and H. Breuer, whose landscapes are eagerly sought for, and command high prices. The frequent sales of paintings are the best evidence that the people of San Francisco equal the citizens of the oldest cities of the land in refinement and the elevation of the mind and heart above the mere desire to make money. There is also a goodly array of female artists who deserve praise and honour. Eastern cities must look well to their laurels in the matter of art as well as in many other things. The contrast between 1849 and 1901 in the prices paid for articles of consumption and service rendered is quite remarkable. When Bayard Taylor visited San Francisco in 1849 he paid the sum of two dollars to a Mexican porter to carry his trunk from the ship to the Plaza or Portsmouth Square. Here in an adobe building, he tells us, he had his lodging. His bed, in a loft, and his three meals per day, consisting of beefsteak, bread and coffee, cost him thirty-five dollars a week. From other sources we learn that, if you kept house, you had to pay fifty cents per pound for potatoes, - one might weigh a pound. Apples were sold at fifty cents a piece, dried apples at seventy-five cents a pound. Fresh beef cost fifty cents a pound, milk was a dollar a quart, hens brought six dollars a piece, eggs nine dollars a dozen, and butter brought down from Oregon, was sold at the rate of two dollars and fifty cents per pound. Flour was in demand at fifty dollars a barrel, and a basket of greens would readily bring eight dollars. A cow cost two hundred dollars. A tin coffee pot was worth five dollars, and a small cooking stove was valued at one hundred dollars. A cook commanded three hundred dollars a month, a clerk two hundred dollars a month, and a carpenter received twelve dollars a day. Lumber sold for four hundred dollars per thousand feet, and for a small dwelling house you had to pay a rental of five hundred dollars per month. It must be remembered that people were pouring into San Francisco from all parts of the world in search of gold, that there were few if any persons to till the ground, and that many of the articles in demand for life's necessities were brought either across the Isthmus of Panama or around by Cape Horn. In consequence the cost of living was necessarily high. To-day you can live as cheaply in San Francisco or any other city of California, as Santa Barbara, Los Angeles, or San Diego, as in any eastern city or town. Rooms with board can be secured at the Palace Hotel, corner of Market street and New Montgomery, at the rate of three dollars and a half per day up to five dollars. Without board you can obtain a room for the sum of one dollar and a half up to three dollars. The Grand Hotel, the annex to the Palace, and just across the street, offers the same rates as the Palace. The Lick House, the corner of Montgomery and Sutler streets, will take you for three dollars up to five per day. The Occidental, corner of Montgomery and Bush streets charges also from three dollars up to five per day for board and room. The California Hotel, an imposing structure, on Bush street, supplies rooms at the rate of one dollar per day and upwards. The Baldwin, corner of Market and Powell streets, charges for board and room at the rate of two dollars and a half up to five per day; and the Russ House receives guests, giving room and board at the rate of one dollar and a half up to two dollars and a half per day - this hotel is situated on the corner of Montgomery and Pine streets. There are many other hotels where the traveller can be made comfortable at a moderate cost. It is the same with many private houses which are open for guests. In the latter a parlor and bedroom with the luxury of a bath may be had for two dollars per day. A single room can be secured for a dollar a day. In such a case you can obtain your meals at one of the numerous restaurants for which San Francisco is noted. There are the restaurants at the Palace, the California and other prominent hotels, the Maison Doree in Kearney street, Westerfeldt's in Market street, and the Cafe in the Call Building on the top floor of the tower, from which you have a commanding view of the city in all directions. Good servants can be had at the rate of thirty dollars per month, especially the much abused Chinese, who cook and do the laundry work, and wait on the table, and render a willing service. I recall the faithfulness of the Chinaman "Fred," who tried to please his employer, and also the fidelity and zeal of "Max," the Dane, or Mads Christensen. Max was an ideal waiter. He had been only nine months in the United States, and yet he had learned sufficient of the English language to understand what was said to him and to express himself clearly. It is an example of persistence; and Max had the qualities which, in a young man, are bound to lead to success.

In addition to the other great buildings you cannot fail to notice the New City Hall, a magnificent pile including the Hall of Records to the east of the main structure. The location is somewhat central, being opposite Eighth street, just north of Market street, and bounded by Park avenue, Larkin and McAllister streets. The plot of ground on which it is erected has an area of six and three-quarters acres and is triangular in shape. The front is eight hundred feet in length, the Larkin street side five hundred and fifty feet, and the McAllister side six hundred and fifty feet long. While the architecture is difficult to describe, as being of any particular order, yet it may be said that it is partly classical, partly of the renaissance style and that it has a suggestion of the Byzantine period, which is seen in so many buildings of a public character. Nothing, however, could be more dignified than this great and imposing structure, which is traversed by a main corridor crossed by a central one with two others, one in the east and the other in the west. These corridors which give you a sense of amplitude, are paved with Vermont marble. It has one chief dome, three hundred feet above the base, which is surmounted by a colossal figure with a torch in the uplifted right hand, a goddess of liberty. On another section of the Hall is a small tower with a flag staff, then a lower dome with a flag staff, the dome being supported by pillars with Corinthian capitals. Flowers were in bloom in the court-yards the day when I visited the building, and they gave an artistic appearance to the granite-foundations. The upper courses of the Hall are made of stucco in imitation of granite. The building, which was begun in 1870, was completed in 1895. What it cost is hard to tell. I questioned several persons in regard to it, but received different answers, ranging all the way from five millions of dollars up to thirteen millions. San Francisco, however, may well be proud of the white edifice, in which are located most of the offices relating to the business of the city. But we must not depart from these precincts until we have examined the monumental group in the New City Hall Square on the south side or front. The monument is circular in form and is crowned with a figure of a woman, representing California, in bronze. She wears a chaplet made of olive leaves, and holds a wand in her right hand, and in her left a large disk bordered with stars, while a bear is seen standing on her right side. No doubt Bruin has reference to the famous bear flag which had been raised on the Plaza in 1846, when California declared herself independent of Mexico, and which in the same year gave place to the Stars and Stripes. Around the monumental figure of California are subjects in bronze. First of all there is an overland wagon drawn by oxen, with pioneers accompanying it. Secondly an Indian wigwam with hunters and Indians representing the year 1850. In the third scene we have a buffalo hunt, the hunter holding a lasso in his hand, and then there is the dying buffalo. Succeeding this we have a domestic scene - fruits and wheat - and a reaper in 1848. We then note bronze-medallions of Sutter, James Lick, Fremont, Drake, the American Flag, and Serra. Moreover on this central monument we have the names of Stockton, Castro, Vallejo, Marshall, Sloat, Larkin, Cabrillo-Portalo. Then the date, "Erected A.D. 1894. Dedicated to the City of San Francisco by James Lick."

The scenes on the four monuments around the central one are - First, the finding of gold in '"49" - three miners. Second, a figure with an oar. Third, Early Days. Indian with bow and arrow. Pioneer with saddle and lasso. A Franciscan preaching. Fourth, a figure crowned with wheat, apples in right hand, and the Horn of plenty with various fruits in the left hand. The monument bears this inscription, near the base - Whyte and De Rome, Founders. Frank Appersberger, Sculptor.

In front of this most interesting monument is a cannon that has a history. Near the head of this instrument of destruction is the legend, *Pluribus nec Impar*. On the body of the cannon we read Le Prince De Conde. *Ultima Ratio Regum*. Louis Charles De Bourbon - Comte D'Eu., Due D'Aumale. A Douay - Par T. Berenger. Commissionaire. Des Fontes Le 23 Mars, 1754.

The cannon is made of bronze, has a coat of arms, and is otherwise ornamented. It has two handles in the shape of dragons. It is twelve feet long. But it has another inscription in which we are deeply interested. This is in English, and reads as follows:

"Captured at Santiago De Cuba, July 17, 1898, by the Fifth Army Corps, U.S. Army, Commanded by Major General William R. Shafter, and presented by him to the City of San Francisco, California, in trust for the Native Sons of the Golden West, and accepted as a token of the valor and patriotism of the Army of the United States."

While I was reading the inscriptions and making measurements an open two-seated carriage was driven up to the curbstone, about four o'clock in the afternoon. From this a gentleman in a business suit, about sixty years of age, alighted and approached me. He was a man of pleasing address. He said to me, "You seem to be interested in this cannon." "I am," was the reply. Then he began to pace it and to examine it, and said, "It is just twelve feet long." He thought that possibly it came into the hands of the Spaniards during the Napoleonic wars, and that it at length found its way over to Cuba to help in enslaving the people of that island. As I was attracted to my informant, I ventured to ask him whom I had the pleasure of addressing. Imagine my astonishment and delight when he said modestly - "I am General Shafter." I said to him, "I am glad to meet one so brave and who has helped to add new lustre to our Flag." He replied that "he considered it a privilege to have had a share in the liberation of Cuba, and that our beloved nation was on the march to still greater glory." Finding out where I came from, and that I lived near Ballston Spa, he said, "You must know my son-in-law, William H. McKittrick." I replied that I did, that I knew him when he was a boy, and that he and his family were my parishioners, when I was Rector of Christ Church, Ballston Spa, twenty-eight years ago. Said he, "William distinguished himself in the Cuban War. He is now a Captain and Assistant Adjutant-General, and it was he who was the first to hoist the Flag over Santiago." The General having courteously invited me to call on him, soon after bade me good-bye. It was a chance meeting, but full of interest, especially under the circumstances. Here was the hero who had captured the cannon and who had won laurels for himself and for his country. McKittrick also comes of a patriotic family, his father having laid his life on the altar of his country in the Civil War; and after the elder McKittrick is named the Grand Army Post of Ballston Spa, N.Y. - Post McKittrick. General Shafter was as modest on the day when I met him by the cannon as he was brave at Santiago. While the Republic has such worthy sons she has nothing to fear. Her mission is one of peace to her own people in all the States and Territories of the Union, and in all our Colonial possessions; and the motto of every citizen should be *Non sibi sed Patriae*. For every churchman it ought to be *Non sibi sed Ecclesiae*.

CHAPTER VII

CHINAMEN OF SAN FRANCISCO - THEIR CALLINGS AND CHARACTERISTICS

A Visit to Chinatown - Its Boundaries - A Terra Incognita - Fond of Mongrels - My Licensed Guide - The Study of the Signs - Men of All Callings - Picture of the Chinaman - Devoid of Humour - Confucius – Great Men from Good Mothers - Confucius to Women - Mormonism and Mohammedanism - How to Regenerate China - Slaves of the Lamp - Chinamen Impassive - Aroused to Wrath - How They Dress - The Queue - "Pidgin" English - Payment of Debts - Bankrupt Law - Suicide.

When in the City of the Golden Gate you will not fail to visit the Chinese Quarter, or "Chinatown," as it is popularly called. Just as in an Oriental city like Jerusalem or Constantinople you find different nationalities or races living apart from each other, so here in San Francisco you have "Little China" in the heart of Anglo-Saxon civilisation. It is as if you had unfolded to your wondering eyes in a dream some town from the banks of the Pearl River, the Yangtse-Kiang, or the Hwangho or. Yellow River; and it seems strange indeed that, without the trouble or expense and danger of crossing the waters of the Pacific, you can by a short walk from the midst of the teeming life of an

American City, be ushered into streets that are foreign in appearance and where scenes that are unfamiliar to the eye attract your attention on every hand. With the exception of the houses, which, as a rule, take on a European or an American style of architecture, you might imagine that you were in Canton or some other Chinese city. The life is truly Asiatic and Mongolian in its character and in its display as well as in its customs. The home of the sons of the Flowery Kingdom in San Francisco is in the north-eastern section of the city, and may be said to be in one of the best portions of the metropolis of the West, sheltered as it is from the winds of the Pacific by the hills which are back of it, and with a commanding view of the Bay and its islands and the magnificent landscapes to the east, valleys and hills running up to the heights of the Sierras. The locality is bounded by Jackson, Pacific, Dupont, Commercial, and Sacramento streets, and embraces some eight squares; and within this space, crowded together, are the twenty-five or thirty thousand Chinese who form a part of the population of the city. There are Chinamen here and there in other parts of San Francisco, but nearly all live here in this quarter which we are now approaching. Here there are the homes of the people who came from the land of Confucius, here the famous shops, the theatres, the Joss-houses where heathen worship is maintained. As soon then as you set foot within the area described you feel that you are in a strictly foreign country; and if this is your first visit, the place is to you a sort of terra incognita. You will need a guide to take you through its labyrinths and point out to you its hidden recesses and explain the strange sights and interpret for you the language which sounds so oddly to your ears. If you have not some man to conduct you, a dragoman or courier, you will be likely to make mistakes as ludicrous as that related of an English woman. Sir Henry Howarth, the author of the "History of the Mongols," a learned and laborious work, was out dining one evening. It fell to his lot at his host's house to escort a lady to the dinner table; and she, having a confused idea of the great man's theme, surprised him somewhat by the abrupt question, "I understand, Sir Henry, that you are fond of dogs. Are you not? I am too." "Dogs, madam? I really must plead guiltless. I know nothing at all of them!" "Indeed," his fair questioner replied; "and they told me you had written a famous history of mongrels!" It is best then always to take a guide, and you will have no trouble in finding one, who will charge you from two to three dollars an hour. If you go with a small party, which is best, all can share the expense. It will take about three hours to explore the town thoroughly and study the life. The writer went through Chinatown on two evenings at an interval of a few days, and saw this Asiatic Quarter of San Francisco to great advantage. The first time was with a licensed guide of long experience, and the second time it was under the direction of a police-detective. Some five friends were in the party; and we started on our tour of exploration about half past nine o'clock at night. The night is the best time in which to study the life, for then you can see the Chinese in their houses and at their amusements, as well as many others who still are at work; for some of the Chinese artisans toil for sixteen hours a day, and long into the hours of the night. Here among them are no strikes for fewer hours, but patient toil, as it were in a treadmill, without a murmur. My licensed guide was Henry Gehrt, a man about fifty-five years old, of German parentage. He had been in the business for twenty-seven years, and he maintained an office on Sacramento Street. His badge was No. 60. All guides must wear badges according to law. As we went hither and thither we met occasionally groups of sight-seers, among them some of our friends, members of the Convention, Bishops, and clerical and lay deputies, who felt this was a rare opportunity to study heathendom; and I am sure all went away from this strange spot thanking God for our noble Anglo-Saxon civilisation, as well as for the knowledge of His Revelation.

The houses, I observed, are three, and sometimes four stories high, with balconies and windows, which give them a decidedly Oriental appearance. On most of them were signs displayed in the Chinese language. You also see scrolls by the doors of the private houses and on the shops. The signs are a study in their bright colours and their mythological and fantastic adornments. Yellow is the predominant colour, and the dragon is in evidence everywhere. This emblem of the Celestial Empire is represented in gorgeous array and with a profusion of ornament. A splendid dragon is the sign and trade mark of "Sing Fat and Co.," who keep a Chinese and Japanese Bazaar on Dupont Street. On their card they give this warning, "Beware of firms infringing on our name;" and it seems as if the dragon on the sign would avenge any invasion of their rights. The signs are a study, and if you are ignorant of the language, you ask your learned guide to interpret them for you. He will tell you that Hop Wo does business here as a grocer, that Shun Wo is the butcher, that Shan Tong is the tea-merchant, that Tin Yuk is the apothecary, and that Wo-Ki sells bric-a-brac. Some of the signs, your guide will tell you, are not the real names of the men who do business, that they are only mottoes. Wung Wo Shang indicates to you that perpetual concord begets wealth, Hip Wo speaks to you of brotherly love and harmony, Tin Yuk means a jewel from Heaven, Wa Yun is the fountain of flowers, while Man Li suggests thousands of profits. Other of the signs relate to the muse. They do not at all reveal the business carried on within. The butcher, for example, has over his shop such elegant phrases as Great Concord, Constant Faith, Abounding Virtue. There are many pawn-brokers who ply their vocation assiduously. They tell you of their honest purpose after this fashion: "Let each have his due pawn-brokers," and, "Honest profit pawn-brokers." In the Chinese restaurant, to which we will go later, you will be edified by such sentiments as these, - The Almond-Flower Chamber, Chamber of the Odours of Distant Lands, Garden of the Golden Valley, Fragrant Tea-Chamber. The apothecary induces you to enter his store with inviting signs of this character: Benevolence and Longevity Hall, Hall of Everlasting Spring, Hall of Joyful Relief, Hall for Multiplying Years. Surely if the American druggist would exhibit such sentences as these over his shop he would never suffer for want of customers. All are in pursuit of length of years and health; and I think the Chinese pharmacist shows his great wisdom in offering to all who are suffering from the ills to which flesh is heir a panacea for their ailments. It takes the fancy, it is a pleasing conceit for the mind, and the mere thought that you are entering Longevity Hall gives you fresh courage!

You will find here in Chinatown men of all callings, the labourer who is ready to bear any burden you lay on him, the artisan who is skilled in his work, the grocer, the clothes' dealer, the merchant, the apothecary, the doctor, the tinsmith, the furniture-maker, the engraver, the goldsmith, the maker of paper-shrines for idols, the barber, the clairvoyant, the fortune-teller, and all others of every calling which is useful and brings profit to him who pursues it. But we are deeply interested in the men whom we meet. At first view they all seem to look alike, you can hardly distinguish one from another. They are a study. Look on their solemn faces, sphinx-like in their repose and imperturbability. They are a riddle to you. You rarely ever hear them laugh. They are like a landscape beneath skies which are wanting in the sparkling sunbeams. They seem to you as if they had continual sorrow of heart, as if some wrong of past ages had set its seal on their features. The Chinaman has very little sense of the ludicrous, and he is lacking in the elements of intellectual sprightliness and vivacity which lead a Frenchman or an American to appreciate and enjoy a sally of wit, a bon mot, or a joke. Life indeed is better, and a man can bear his burdens with more ease if he has a sense of humour. Some of the great characters in history have often come out of the depths with triumph by reason of the spirit within them which could perceive the flash of wit and apply its medicine to the wounds of the heart. I think it may be said, as a rule, that the Asiatic has not the power to appreciate wit and humour like the old Greek or the Teuton or the Celt. He is not wanting in his love of the beautiful, in his appreciation of poetry, in the vision which perceives the flowers blooming by the waters in the desert, and in the hearing which catches the sound of the harmonies of his palm-trees and lotus flowers, but in the sense or faculty to seize on mirth and appropriate her to his service in burden-bearing he is sadly deficient. He is but a child in this respect. While the Chinaman has inventive faculties and keen intellect and wonderful imitative powers, yet in other respects he is behind the progressive races of the world. He has made little advance for thousands of years. His isolation, his narrow sphere, his simple life, and his religion even, which, while some of its maxims and tenets are admirable, still is lacking in the knowledge of the true God and in lofty ideals, have had a marked effect upon his thoughts and habits and pursuits. His great teacher, Confucius, who flourished five centuries before the Christian era and who spoke some sublime truths, was nevertheless ignorant of a Revelation from heaven and inferior in his grasp of religious truth to such sages of Greece as Socrates and Plato. In his system also woman is practically a slave. She is simply the minister of man, and therefore unable to rear up children, sons who would reflect the greatness of soul of a noble motherhood. It has often been remarked that great men have had great mothers. I think experience and observation will bear out this statement. Glance over the pages of history, and eminent examples will rise up before the view. Whence spring the Samuels and the Davids, whence a Leonidas and a Markos Bozzaris, whence the Scipios and the Gracchi, whence the Augustines and the Chrysostoms, whence the Alfreds and the Gladstones, whence the Washingtons and the Lincolns, whence the Seaburys and the Doanes, and many another? Are they not all hewn from the quarries of a noble motherhood? Are they not sprung from the fountain of a womanhood whose living streams are clear as crystal and sweet and refreshing? The first Chavah, Eve, is rightly styled the mother of all living; and a generation or race of men to be living, active, noble in achievement, distinguished in virtues, must issue from a well-spring which vitalises and beautifies and magnifies the spirit and the intellect, as Engannim waters her gardens, and Engedi nourishes her acacias and lotus-plants, and Enshemesh reflects the sun's golden beams the livelong day. But what, you ask, are the exact teachings of the sage Confucius, who influences Chinese society even to this day, with regard to woman? Hear him: "Moreover, that you have not in this life been born a male is owing to your amount of wickedness, heaped up in a previous state of existence, having been both deep and weighty; you would not then desire to adorn virtue, to heap up good actions, and learn to do well! So that you now have been hopelessly born a female! And if you do not this second time specially amend your faults, this amount of wickedness of yours will be getting both deeper and weightier, so that it is to be feared in the next state of existence, even if you should wish for a male's body, yet it will be very difficult to get it." Again another saying of Confucius is: "You must know that for a woman to be without talent is a virtue on her part." With such teaching then ever before them, do you wonder that Chinese women do not excel in virtue, and that they are the mothers of a race of men who are practically like standing water instead of a flowing fountain to refresh the waste places of human life? The teachings of Mormonism and Mohammedanism with regard to woman also degrade her and rob her of the beautiful crown which her Maker has put upon her head; and hence it is that such peoples are not virile and progressive like the nations where woman is looked upon as man's helpmeet, where she stands upon his right hand as a queen. The Mormons are better in many respects than their faith; and if the first generation was hardy and aggressive and brave in subduing the desert and changing Rocky Mountain wastes into a blooming garden, it was because they had been trained in the school of Christianity and had imbibed lessons of wisdom at the fountain of a pure faith and inherited from Christian fathers and mothers those qualities which are stamped on the soul through upright living and a creed that is formulated in true doctrine. But Mormonism is dying out, and woman in

Utah is receiving the rightful place assigned her by her Creator in the work of building up the race and perpetuating the virtues and forces of a true manhood. The followers of Mohammed are still numerous and powerful, and the Religion of the Koran has shown great vitality for centuries. The nobility of character, however, which has manifested itself in such lives as that of Saladin the Great is the product of other causes than the specific teachings and views of Islam respecting domestic life and the position and office of woman. The destinies of men have been determined often by their environments. We must also bear in mind that from time to time, under the sway of the Crescent, different sections of the civilised world have been brought under the rule of the Sultans, and all that was good and noble in the lives of peoples newly incorporated into the faith of the Arabian Prophet has contributed in no small degree to the strength of a system which has in its own bosom the seeds of decay and which will ultimately become effete and pass away. Mohammed Ali, the founder of the present Khedivial house of Egypt, had in his veins old Macedonian blood, and his views respecting marriage and domestic life, as well as the traditions of his family in his old home at Kavala, had much to do with the development of his character and his brilliant career; and hence neither he nor others like him in the Turkish Empire can be singled out to prove that a religion which looks upon woman as an inferior being to man is excellent in its tendencies and produces a noble fruitage. What Napoleon once said with respect to France, that she needed good mothers, is true as regards China. Where woman is held in honour and where the domestic virtues are woven into a beautiful chaplet of spring-time blossoms to bedeck her brow, there you will find good and great men. Our own nation is an example of this. To regenerate China then, to improve the morals of Chinatown in San Francisco, or Chinatown in New York where there are between seven and eight thousand sons and daughters of the Flowery Kingdom, you must create pure homes, and to do this you must first of all sweeten them with the precepts of the Gospel of Jesus Christ. Confucius will fail you. The Son of God will reform you and save you! Such thoughts and reflections as these naturally sprang up in my mind in my walks through Chinatown. I saw its people on every hand. Sometimes they were in twos, again in groups of a half a dozen or more. They scarcely noticed us as we walked by them; they showed no curiosity to observe us, but went on their way as though intent on one object. They moved about like automatons, as if they were a piece of machinery; and such as were at work in shops heeded us not even when we stood over them and watched them as they handled their tools. It was work, work. They were doing their masters' bidding like the genii of the lamp; and in the glare of the light in which they wrought on their bench or at their stand the workers in gold and silver, the makers of ornaments and jewelry, were like some strange beings from another world. They work to the point of endurance. They have their amusements, their holidays, as the Chinese New Year which comes in February, their processions from time to time, but their great indulgence is in the use of opium. Once or twice a month the ordinary labourer or workman gives himself up to its seductive charms, to its power more fatal to his manhood than intoxicating drinks taken to excess. The Chinaman is so stolid and impassive that it is hard to arouse his wrath. He will bear insults without a murmur for a long time, but in the end he will be stung into madness and he will give force to all his pent up fires of hate that have slumbered like a volcano. He may wait long without having punished his oppressor, but he will bide his time. So it was with the Boxers in China whose story is so painfully fresh in the memories of the great legations of the world in Pekin.

The men and women of Chinatown dress very nearly like each other; though you do not meet many women. The Chinaman wears a blouse of blue cotton material or other cheap, manufactured goods. This is without a collar, and is usually hooked over the breast. There are no buttons. Wealthy Chinamen, and there are many such, indulge in richer garments. As a rule they have adopted the American felt hat of a brownish colour. The shoe has the invariable wooden sole with uppers of cotton or some kind of ordinary cloth. The hair is the object of their chief attention, however, in the making up of their toilet. It is worn in a queue or pigtail fashion as it is commonly styled. It is their glory, however, this long, black, glossy braid. It is the Chinaman's distinguishing badge. It gives him dignity in the presence of his countrymen. If cut off he feels dishonoured. He can never go back to the home of his ancestors, but must remain in exile. He wears this mark of his nationality either hanging down his back or else coiled about the head. When at work the latter style is preferred, as it is then out of the way of his movements. Some of the men whom you meet have fine intellectual heads. The merchants and scholars whom I saw answer to this description. As a rule they can all read and write. They have a love of knowledge to a certain point, and a book is prized by them. The great desire of the Chinamen who reach our shores is to learn the English language. They know it gives them an advantage. It is the avenue to success. Sometimes they will become members of an American Mission or

Bible-class in order to learn the language. They still, however, have their mental reservations with regard to their native Joss-houses and worship. But they are not singular in this respect. Mohammedans and Jews in the East allow their children to attend schools where English is taught, because with the knowledge of this they can the more readily find employment among tourists and in places of exchange. This is particularly true in Egypt and in Syria. But the Chinaman in his attempt to learn the Anglo-Saxon tongue finds great difficulties. Very many speak only what is called "Pidgin" or "Pigeon" English, that is Business English. Business on the lips of the new learner becomes "Pidgin." They like to end a word with ee as "muchee," and they find it next to impossible to frame the letter R. For example the word *rice* becomes *lice* in a Chinaman's mouth, and a Christian is a Chlistian, while an American is turned into an Amelican. Of course this does not apply to the educated Chinaman who is polished and gifted in speech as is the case with any well-trained Chinese clergyman or such as minister Wu Ting-Fang in Washington.

All debts among the Chinese are paid once a year, that is when their New Year comes around in our month of February. There are three ways in which they may cancel their debts. First, they pay them in money, if they are able, when accounts are cast up between creditor and debtor. If in the second place they are unable to pay what they owe they assign all their goods and effects to their creditors, and then the debtor gets a clean bill and so starts out anew with a clear conscience for another year. This in few words is the Chinese "Bankrupt Law." But, in the third place, if a man has no assets, if he be entirely impoverished, and cannot pay his debts, he considers it a matter of honour to kill himself. Death pays all debts for him, settles all scores, and he is not looked upon with aversion or execrated. Even Chinese women have resorted to this extreme method of settling their accounts. But what of their settlement with their Maker who gave them life, who holds all men responsible for that gift, who expects us to use the boon aright? A Chinaman does not value life with the same feeling and estimate as an Anglo-Saxon. Should he fail in any great purpose, should he meet with defeat in some cherished plan, he will seek refuge in the bosom of the grave; he will voluntarily return to his ancestors whom he has worshipped as gods. In the late war between China and Japan, in which China was vanquished, some of her generals committed suicide. It presents, alas, a degenerate side of human nature. It is most pathetic. Better far to live under the smart of defeat and bear its shame, carry the cross, endure the stings of conscience, and meet the frowns of the world, than flee from the path of duty, than dishonour our manhood. The greatest victory is to conquer one's proud heart, and to suffer, and do God's will. The teachings of Christ show us the value of life, tell us how to live, how to die, how to win the divine approbation. To Him we bow and not to Confucius.

CHAPTER VIII

A CHINESE NEWSPAPER, LITTLE FEET, AND AN OPIUM JOINT

In Chinatown - A Chinese Editor - His Views of Chinese Life - A Daily Paper and the Way in Which it is Printed - A Night School - The Mission of the English Language - A Widow and Her Children - Pair of Small Shoes - Binding of the Feet and Custom - Mrs. Wu Ting-Fang on Small Feet - Maimed and Veiled Women - The Shulamite's Feet - An Opium-joint - A Wretched Chinaman - Fascination of Opium - History and Cultivation of the Poppy - The East India Company and the Opium War - An Opium Farmer - How the Old Man Smoked - De Quincey and His Experiences - "I Will Sleep No More."

As my guide and I went forth to visit the places of interest in Chinatown, we directed our steps first of all to the Chinese newspaper office. This is located at No. 804 Sacramento street, corner of Dupont street. On being ushered in I met with a cordial welcome from the managing editor, Mr. Ng Poon Chew, who, before I bade him good-bye, exchanged cards with me. He, I learned, is a Christian minister and is the pastor of a Chinese church in Los Angeles. His literary attainments and business capacity peculiarly fit him for his work on the Chinese paper, and he is held in high esteem by Chinamen generally. He is a man about four feet five inches in stature, and possibly forty years old. It is hard, however, to tell a Chinaman's age, and so he may be five or ten years older. He is what you would call a handsome man, with a fine head and a beaming countenance. He showed great warmth in his greeting - and this was the more remarkable as the Chinaman is generally cool and impassive. He was dressed in the Chinese fashion with the traditional queue hanging down behind. He presented altogether a striking appearance, and you would single him out from a crowd as a man of more than ordinary cultivation and ability. He talked English fluently, and it was a pleasure to listen to him. He has well defined views regarding China and other countries. When questioned about the Flowery Kingdom, he said that the people were very conservative, that they do not wish for change, and that Chinese women dress as they did thousands of years ago. He remarked, however, that there is a younger generation of Chinamen who long for a change and for reform in methods, I suppose after the manner of the so-called "Young Turks" in the Sultan's dominions. They would like the improvements of European and American life, and would shake off the trammels of the past to a large extent, just as Japan has shaken off the sleep of centuries and is marching towards greatness among the strong nations of the world. With the modern appliances and advances in civilisation and armies well drilled like those of England or the United States of America, and with great war-ships well manned, they would be able to meet the world and to defend themselves and repel every invader from their country. He says the Chinese have good memories, that they will never forget the manner in which opium came to them, and the opium war of 1839. When he was a child he was taught to pray to a wooden god, and he had to rise as early as 3:30 A.M. to go to school to study the teachings of Confucius. As the custom is to go so early in the morning to school, the children sometimes drop to sleep by the way as they are hastening on. Chinamen will tell you that they have the religion which is best for them. This is the doctrine of Confucius; but Confucius, while a great scholar, was not a saint. He taught men "to improve their pocket," but did not teach them much about their soul. In order to see the real effect of the teachings of Confucius, you must go to China. Confucius may make men whom you may admire, but he cannot make men whom you can respect. The religion of Confucius is dreary and is lacking in the warmth and blessing which come from a belief in the Bible.

It is most certainly refreshing to hear this learned Chinaman talking and giving his impressions and opinions about matters of such vital importance. Ng Poon Chew, at my request, gave me the business card of the newspaper. This states that the paper, which is published daily in Chinese, is called "Chung Sai Yat Po," and that it has the largest circulation of any Chinese paper published outside of the Chinese Empire. The card further tells us that "this paper is the organ of the commercial element in America and is the best medium for Chinese trade." In addition to the daily issue of the newspaper, "English and Chinese Job Printing" is done in the office. The work of interpreting the English and Chinese languages is carried on here. Mr. Ng Poon Chew spoke with evident pride about his paper, and informed me that he gave a daily account of the proceeding's of the General Convention, then in session in Trinity Church, San Francisco, in the "Chung Sai Yat Po."

The editing of a Chinese newspaper is no easy matter. The printing of the paper is difficult and requires great skill and patience. There are, for example, forty thousand word-signs, all different, in the Chinese language, and to represent these signs there must be separate, movable type-pieces. It is said that it takes a long period of time to distribute the type and lay out "the case." The typesetter must know the word by sight to tell its meaning, otherwise he will make serious blunders. Then it is a hard matter to find intelligent typesetters. The editor, too, must be a man of business. The paper is watched by spies of the Chinese Government, and if the editor expresses himself in any manner antagonistic to the Emperor or the Dowager Empress or any of the viceroys of the provinces, his head would be cut off if he ever ventured to set foot in China. There is another obstacle in the way of a Chinese newspaper of liberal views, like the "Chung Sai Yat Po." It cannot get its type from China, as the Government is opposed to every reform paper. The type for such a journal is cast in a Japanese foundry in Yokohama. It is said that about ten thousand word-signs are used in the printing of the newspaper. The type-case is usually long, for the purpose of allowing all the type-pieces to be spread out. The type runs up and down in a column, and you read from right to left as in Hebrew or other Shemitic languages. The characters are as old in form as the days of Confucius. The "Chung Sai Yat Po" has a very large circulation and finds its way to the islands of the Pacific Ocean and into China.

From the newspaper office we wended our way to a little Baptist mission chapel for the Chinese. There were about forty persons congregated here, among them some ten or twelve Americans who were teaching the Chinese the English language. This night school is popular with young, ambitious Chinamen, for when they learn our language it is much easier for them to obtain work in stores and offices, and even as house servants. The books used had the Chinese words on one page and the English sentences opposite. Sometimes converts to Christianity are made through the medium of the night school, but it takes time and patience to win a Chinaman from the religion of Confucius. It is worth the labour, however. The difficulties in the mastery of English are a great barrier to conversions. Nevertheless they do occur. A Chinaman is readily reached through his own language. Hence the importance of raising up native teachers of the Gospel who can speak to the hearts as well as to the understanding of their countrymen. As we observed in the foregoing chapter, in the Orient, as in Syria and Egypt, Jews and Mohammedans sometimes allow their children to attend the English schools, and to a large extent from a worldly motive. The Syrian or Arab who can speak English is in demand as a dragoman, an accountant, an office clerk in the bazaar, or a camp-servant or boatman. Indeed a great revolution is now taking place all through the East. Nearly all the young Egyptians can talk English, and this is the first step towards their conversion to the faith of the Gospel. When they are able to read the books of the Christians in the English, they are led to look favourably on the Church. They catch the spirit of belief in Jesus Christ from the Christian tourist. They lose the narrowness and bigotry which the mosque or the synagogue fosters, and in time they examine the claims of a religion which has built up the great nations of Europe and America. The future has in store great developments for the Church in Palestine and the old land of the Pharaohs through the agency of the

English schools, and I believe the readiest way in which to convert the Chinese people, whether in Chinatown in San Francisco, or in China itself, is to teach them our language and give them access to the Holy Scriptures in our noble tongue. Our Church schools in China are doing a great work in this respect. So is St. John's College in Shanghai. They should all be liberally supported with offerings from America, and what we sow in this generation will be reaped in the next, a splendid harvest for Christ and His Church!

After leaving the night school our guide conducted us up narrow stairs to the rooms occupied by a Chinese woman. She was a widow with four children, daughters, and rather petite in form, and lacking the physical development and beauty of the Caucasian race. They seemed shy and timid, for Chinese women are not accustomed to the society of men. In fact there is among them no such home-life as we are familiar with. They were dressed in a measure after the fashion of our girls, and had long, black hair. The mother said a few sentences in broken English, and welcomed us with an air of sincerity, though not a little embarrassed. She was a woman of about forty years, and from the expression of her face had evidently met with trials. Brought over to San Francisco from Canton when a young girl, she had married Shan Tong with all the ceremony and merry-making which characterise a Chinese wedding, with its processions and feasting and the noise of its firecrackers; but some four or five years ago death claimed her husband, and she was left to do battle alone, while he was laid to rest in the Chinese burying-ground at the west end of Laurel Hill Cemetery. But she did not suffer from want, for Chinamen are kind to the needy of their own race. Among the objects which excited our curiosity were the tiny shoes of the small-footed woman. These were not quite three inches in length, and looked as if they were more suited for a doll's feet than for a full grown woman's. Yes, here was the evidence of a barbarous custom which deprives a human being of one of nature's good gifts, so necessary to our comfort and happiness. Think what you would be, if, through infirmity, you were not at liberty to go hither and thither at will like the young hart or gazelle! We grieve naturally if our children's feet are deformed or misshapen at birth, but what a crime it is to destroy the form and strength of the foot as God has made it! It is true that the Manchu women in China rejoice in the feet which the beneficent Creator has given them. The Dowager Empress - of whom we have read so much of late, and who rules China with an iron rod, has feet like any other woman; but millions of her countrywomen have been robbed of nature's endowment through a foolish and wicked custom which has prevailed in China from time immemorial. The feet are bound when the child is born, and they are never allowed to grow as God designed, as the flower expands into beauty from the bud. Chinese women realise that it is foolish, that it is a deformity, but it is the "custom," and custom prevails. It is like the laws of the Medes and Persians which alter not. Women are powerless under it. It is in vain to a large extent that they oppose it. There is in China an Anti-foot-binding League, which receives the support of men of prominence. Even centuries ago imperial edicts were issued against it, but custom still rules. It was Montaigne who declared that "custom" ought to be followed simply because it is custom. A poor reason indeed. There should be a better argument for the doing of what is contrary to reason and nature. Nature is a wise mother, and she bestows on us no member of the body that is unnecessary. The thought of her fostering care was well expressed by the old Greeks who lived an out-door life, in their personification of Mother Earth under the creation of their Demeter, perfect in form and beautiful in expression and noble in action. This is far above the conceptions of nature or of a presiding genius over our lives, taking into account social order and marriage vows, which we find in Chinese literature or mythology. It is not difficult to perceive the reason why the Greeks, who rule the realms of philosophy and art and literature to-day, after the lapse of many centuries, are the superior people. Well does that master-mind, Shakespeare, characterise evil custom:

> "That monster, custom, who all sense doth eat,
> Of habits devil."

But a better day is coming for Chinese women. Wherever Christianity has touched them in the past they have been uplifted and benefited. The sun seems now to rise in greater effulgence on the Kingdom of the Yellow Dragon. The wretched custom of dwarfing and destroying the feet of a child whose misfortune, according to Confucius, it is to be born a female, is giving way under pressure from contact with the enlightened nations of the world. The teachings of the Christian Church are having their salutary effect and Chinamen are beginning to learn the value of a woman's life from the Biblical standpoint, and the daughters of the Flowery Kingdom will, as time goes on, become more and more like the polished corners of the Temple, or the Caryatides supporting the entablature of the Erechtheum at Athens. It is Madame Wu Ting-Fang, wife of the Chinese Minister at Washington, who has recently returned from a visit to her old home, who says: "The first penetrating influence of exterior civilisation on the customs of my country has touched the conditions of women. The emancipation of woman in China means, first of all, the liberation of her feet, and this is coming. Indeed, it has already come in a measure, for the style in feet has changed. Wee bits of feet, those no longer than an infant's, are no longer the fashion. When I went back home I found that the rigid binding and forcing back of the feet was largely a thing of the past. China, with other nations, has come to regard that practice as barbarous, but the small feet, those that enable a woman to walk a little and do not inconvenience her in getting about the house, are still favoured by the Chinese ladies."

The custom of binding and destroying the feet, no doubt, arose from the low views entained by Chinese sages concerning woman, and from a lack of confidence in her sense of honour and virtue. She must be maimed so that she cannot go about at will, so she shall be completely under the eye of her husband, held as it were in fetters. It is a sad comment on Chinese domestic morality, it fosters the very evil it seeks to cure, it destroys all home life in the best sense. The veiled women of the East are very much in the same position. If a stranger, out of curiosity or by accident, look on the face of a Mohammedan wife, it might lead to her repudiation by her jealous husband, or the offender might be punished for his innocent glance. The writer recalls how at Hebron, in Palestine, he was cautioned by the dragoman, when going up a narrow street to the Mosque of Machpelah, where he had to pass veiled women, not to look at them or to seem to notice them, as the men were very fanatical and might do violence to an unwary tourist. The Chinese women of small feet, or rather no feet at all, walk, or attempt to walk, in a peculiar way. It is as if one were on stilts. The feet are nothing but stumps, while the ankles are large, almost unnatural in their development. It is indeed a great deformity. The feet are shrunken to less size than an infant's; but they have not the beauty of a baby's feet, which have in them great possibilities and a world of suggestion and romance and poetry. If the Chinese custom had prevailed among the ancient Hebrew people, think you that King Solomon in singing of the graces of the Shulamite, who represents the Church mystically, would ever have exclaimed, - "How beautiful are thy feet with shoes, O prince's daughter!" We should have lost, moreover, much that is noble in art, and the poetic creations of Greek sculptors would never have delighted the eye nor enchained the fancy.

In our perambulations about Chinatown, we must next visit an opium-joint. This mysterious place was situated in a long, rambling building through which we had to move cautiously so as not to stumble into some pit or dangerous hole or trap-door. Here were no electric lights to drive away the gloom, here no gas-jets to show us where we were treading, nothing but an occasional lamp dimly burning. Yet we went on as if drawn by a magic spell. At last we were ushered into a room poorly furnished. It was not more than twelve feet square, and in the corner was an apology for a bed. On this was stretched an old man whose face was sunken, whose eyes were lusterless, whose hand was long and thin and bony, and whose voice was attenuated and pitched in a falsetto key. The guide said that this old Chinaman was sixty-eight years of age, and that he had had a life of varied experience. He was a miner by profession, but had spent all his earnings long ago, and was now an object of charity as well as of pity. Indeed he was the very embodiment of misery, a wretched, woebegone, human being! He had lost one arm in an accident during his mining days. Chinamen in the thirst for gold had mining claims as well as Anglo-Saxons. This desire for the precious metal seems to be universal. All men more or less love gold; and for its acquisition they will undergo great hardship, face peril, risk their lives. This aged Chinaman for whom there was no future except to join his ancestors in another life, was now a pauper notwithstanding all his quest for the treasures of the mines; and his chief solace, if it be comfort indeed to have the senses benumbed periodically, or daily, and then wake up to the consciousness of loss and with a feeling of despair betimes, was in his opium pipe, which he smoked fifty times a day at the cost of half a dollar, the offering of charity, the dole received from his pitying countrymen or the interested traveller who might come to his forlorn abode. But what a fascination the opium drug has for the Chinaman, and not for him alone, but for children of other races - for men and women who, when under its spell, will sell honour and sacrifice all that is dear in life, and even forego the prospect and the blessed hope of entering at last into the bliss of the heavenly world! But what is opium, what its parentage and history? The Greeks will tell you it is their opion or opos, the juice of the poppy, and the botanist will point out the magic flower for you as the Papaver Somniferum, whose home was originally in the north of Europe and in Western Asia; but now, just as the tribes of the earth have spread out into many lands, so has the poppy which has brought much misery as well as blessing to men, found its way into various quarters of the globe, particularly those countries which are favoured with sunny skies. It is cultivated in Turkey, India, Persia, Egypt, Algeria and Australia, as well as in China. I now recall vividly the beautiful poppy fields at Assiut, Esneh and Kenneh, by the banks of the Nile, in which such subtle powers were sleeping potent for ill or good as employed by man for deadening his faculties or soothing pain in reasonable measure. These flowers were of the reddish kind. In China they have the white, red and purple varieties, which, as you gaze on them, seem to set the fields aglow with fire and attract your gaze as if you were enchained to the spot by an unseen power. The seeds are sown in November and December, in rows which are eighteen inches apart, and four-fifths of the opium used in China is the home-product, though it was not so formerly. In March or April the poppy flowers according to the climate, the soil, and the location. The opium is garnered in April or May, and prepared for the market. The Chinese merchant values most of all the Shense drug, while the Ynnan and the Szechuen drugs take next rank. The opium is generally made into flat cakes and wrapped up in folds of white paper. It is said that it was introduced into China in the reign of Taitsu, between the years A.D. 1280 and 1295; but it is worthy of note that up to the year 1736 it was imported only in small quantities and employed simply for its medicinal properties, as a cure for diarrhoea, dysentery, and fevers, hemorrhage and other ills. It was in the year 1757 that the monopoly of the cultivation of the poppy in India passed into the hands of the East India Company through the victory of Lord Clive over the Great Mogul of Bengal at Plassey; and from this time the importation of the drug into China became a matter of great profit financially. In 1773 the whole quantity imported was only two hundred chests. In 1776 it had increased to one thousand chests, while in 1790 it leaped up to four thousand and fifty-four chests. The Chinese Emperor, Keaking, becoming alarmed at its growing use and its pernicious effect when eaten or smoked, forbade its importation, and passed laws punishing persons who made use of it otherwise than medicinally, and the extreme penalty was sometimes transportation, and sometimes death. Yet the trade increased, and in the decade between 1820 and 1830 the importation was as high as sixteen thousand, eight hundred and seventy-seven chests. The evil became so great that in 1839 a royal proclamation was put forth threatening English opium ships with confiscation if they did not keep out of Chinese waters. This was not heeded, and then Lin, the Chinese Commissioner, gave orders to destroy twenty thousand, two hundred and ninety-one chests of opium, each containing 149-1/3 pounds, the valuation of which was $10,000,000. Still the work of smuggling went on and the result was what is known as the Opium War, which was ended in 1842 by the treaty of Nanking. China was forced by Great Britain to pay $21,000,000 indemnity, to cede in perpetuity to England the city of Hong Kong, and to give free access to British ships entering the ports of Canton, Amoy, Foochoofoo, Ningpo and Shanghai. The importation of opium from India is still carried on - but the quantity is not so great as formerly, owing to the cultivation of the plant in China. The Hong Kong government has an opium farm, for which to-day it receives a rental of $15,500 per month. The farmer sells on an average from eight to ten *tins* of opium daily, the tins being worth about $150 each. His entire receipts from his sales of the drug are about $45,000 per month. This opium farmer is well known to be the largest smuggler of opium into China; and not without reason does Lord Charles Beresford, in his book "The Break-up of China," say: "Thus, indirectly the Hong Kong government derives a revenue by fostering an illegitimate trade with a neighbouring and friendly

Power, which cannot be said to redound to the credit of the British Government. It is in direct opposition to the sentiments and tradition of the laws of the British Empire." It was here in Chinatown, in San Francisco, that I was brought face to face with the havoc that is made through the opium trade and the use of the pernicious drug in eating and smoking. I was told that Europeans and Americans sometimes sought the opium-joints for the purpose of indulgence in the vice of smoking. Even women were known to make use of it in this way. The old man whom I visited was lying on his left side, with his head slightly raised on a hard pillow covered with faded leather. He took the pipe in his right hand, the other, as I have already said, having been cut off in the mines. Then he laid down the pipe by his side with the stem near his mouth. The next movement was to take a kind of long rod, called a dipper, with a sharp end and a little flattened. This he dipped in the opium which had the consistency of thick molasses. He twisted the dipper round and then held the drop which adhered to it over the lamp, which was near him. He wound the dipper round and round until the opium was roasted and had a brown colour. He then thrust the end of the dipper with the prepared drug into the opening of the pipe, which was somewhat after the Turkish style with its long stem. He next held the bowl of the pipe over the lamp until the opium frizzled. Then putting the stem of the pipe in his mouth he inhaled the smoke, and almost immediately exhaled it through the mouth and nostrils. While smoking he removed the opium, going through the same process as before, and it all took about fifteen minutes. What the old man's feelings were he did not tell us, but he seemed very contented, as if then he cared for nothing, as if he had no concern for the world and its trials. But one must read the graphic pages of Thomas De

Quincey in his "Confessions of an English Opium Eater," in order to know what are the joys and what the torments of him who is addicted to the use of the pernicious drug. It was while De Quincey was in Oxford that he came under its tyranny. At first taken to allay neuralgic pain, and then resorted to as a remedy on all occasions of even the slightest suffering, it wove its chain around him like a merciless master who puts his servant in bonds. But though given to its use all his life afterwards, in later years he took it moderately. Still he was its slave. A man of marvellous genius, a master of the English tongue, he had not full mastery of his own appetite; and one of such talent, bound Andromeda-like to the rock of his vice, ready to be devoured in the sea of his perplexity by what is worse than the dragon of the story, he deserves our pity, nay, even our tears. He tells us how he was troubled with tumultuous dreams and visions, how he was a participant in battles, strifes; and how agonies seized his soul, and sudden alarms came upon him, and tempests, and light and darkness; how he saw forms of loved ones who vanished in a moment; how he heard "everlasting farewells;" and sighs as if wrung from the caves of hell reverberated again and again with "everlasting farewells." "And I awoke in struggles, and cried aloud, 'I will sleep no more!'"

CHAPTER IX

MUSIC, GAMBLING, EATING, THEATRE-GOING

In Chinatown - A Musician's Shop - A Secret Society - Gambling Houses - "The Heathen Chinee" - Fortune-telling - The Knife in the Fan-Case - A Boarding House - A Lesson for Landlords - A Kitchen - A Goldsmith's Shop - The Restaurant - Origin of the Tea-Plant - What a Chinaman Eats - The Tobacco or Opium Pipe - A Safe with Eight Locks - The Theatre - Women by Themselves - The Play - The Stage - The Actors - The Orchestra and the Music - The Audience - A Death on the Stage - The Theatre a Gathering Place - No Women Actors - A Wise Provision - Temptations - Real Acting - Men the Same Everywhere.

The reader will now accompany us to a musician's shop in our wanderings through Chinatown. This is located in a basement and is a room about fifteen feet wide and some twenty feet deep. This son of Jubal from the Flowery Kingdom was about fifty-five years old and a very good-natured man. He received us with a smile, and when he was requested by the guide to play for us he sat down before an instrument somewhat like the American piano, called *Yong Chum*. The music was of a plaintive character, and was lacking in the melody of a Broadwood or a Steinway. Then he played on another instrument which resembled a bandore or banjo and was named *Sem Yim*. Afterwards he took up a Chinese flute and played a tune, which was out of the ordinary and was withal of a cheerful nature. He then showed us something that was striking and peculiar - a Chinese fiddle with two strings. The bow strings were moved beneath the fiddle strings. The music was by no means such as to charm one, and you could not for a moment imagine that you were listening to a maestro playing on a Cremona. The Chinese, while they have a reputation for philosophy after the example of their great men, like Confucius and Mencius, and while there are poets of merit among them like Su and Lin, yet can not be said to excel in musical composition and rendering. The tune with which our Chinese friend sought to entertain us on his fiddle was, "A Hot Time in the Old Town To-night." He thought this would be agreeable to our American ears. Meanwhile I glanced around this music-room and among other things I saw, and which interested me, were several effigies of men, characters in Chinese history. Some were no doubt true to life while others were caricatures of the persons whom they represented. It might be styled an Eden Musee.

Leaving the musician's, after giving him a suitable fee for entertaining us, we turned our footsteps towards the *Chee Kung Tong*. This is a Chinese secret society. The Chinese are wont to associate themselves together, even if they do not mingle much with men of other nations. They have their gatherings for social purposes and for improvement and pastime, and, like the Anglo-Saxon and the Latin races, they have their mystic signs and passwords. Of course we were not permitted to enter the *Chee Kung Tong* Hall, however much we desired to cross its mysterious threshold. The door was well guarded, and Chinamen passing in had to give assurance that they were entitled to the privilege. On the night when the detective from Police Headquarters accompanied us we made an attempt to enter a Chinese gambling house. The entrance even to this was well guarded; although the sentinel unwittingly left the door open for a moment as a Chinaman was passing in. The detective seeing his opportunity went in boldly and bade us to follow him. In a few moments all was confusion. We heard hurrying feet in the adjoining room, and then excited men appeared at the head of the passage way and waved their arms to and fro while they talked rapidly in high tones. Outside already some fifty men had collected together, and these were also talking and gesticulating wildly. The detective then said to us that it would be wise to retreat and leave the place lest we might meet with violence. We did so, but the uproar among the Chinese did not subside for some time. We pitied the poor sentinel who had allowed us to slip in, for we knew that he would be severely punished after our departure. The Chinese are noted for their gambling propensities, and there are many gambling houses in Chinatown. This vice is one of their great pastimes, and whenever they are not engaged in business they devote themselves either to gambling, the amusements of the theatre, the pleasures of the restaurant, or the seductive charms of the opium pipe.

Later in my saunterings I went into a kind of restaurant, where I saw a number of Chinese men and boys playing cards and dominoes and dice. They went on with the games as if they were oblivious to us. I noticed there were Chinese coins of small value on the tables, and some of the players were apparently winning while others were losing. The latter, however, gave no indication that they were in the least degree disappointed. Of course, as a rule they play after their own fashion, having their own games and methods. Minister Wu, of Washington, when asked recently if he liked our American games, replied that he did not understand any of them. No doubt this is true of the majority of Chinamen in the United States. In thinking of the Chinese and gambling one always recalls Bret Harte's "Plain Language From Truthful James of Table Mountain," popularly known as "The Heathen Chinee," one of the best humorous poems in the English language. You can fairly see the merry eyes of the author of the "Argonauts of '49" dancing with pleasure as he describes the game of cards between "Truthful James," "Bill Nye" and "Ah Sin."

"Which we had a small game,
And Ah Sin took a hand;
It was euchre: the same
He did not understand;
But he smiled as he sat by the table
With a smile that was childlike and bland.

"Yet the cards they were stacked
In a way that I grieve,
And my feelings were shocked
At the state of Nye's sleeve,
Which was stuffed full of aces and bowers,
And the same with intent to deceive.

"But the hands that were played
By that heathen Chinee,
And the points that he made.
Were quite frightful to see -
Till at last he put down the right bower,
Which the same Nye had dealt unto me.

> "Then I looked up at Nye,
> And he gazed upon me:
> And he rose with a sigh,
> And said, 'Can this be?
> We are ruined by Chinee cheap labour' -
> And he went for that heathen Chinee."

There are all kinds of jugglers in Chinatown and among them are numerous fortune-tellers. This kind of pastime is as old as the human race, and you find the man who undertakes to reveal to you the secrets of the future among all peoples. The Orientals are always ready to listen to the "neby" or the necromancer or the fakir or the wandering minstrel, who improvises for you and sings for you the good things which are in store for you. We see this tendency among our own people who would have their destiny pointed out by means of a pack of cards, by the reading of the palm of the hand, in the grounds in the tea-cup, and by other signs. It was with some interest then that we glanced at the mystic words and signs which adorned the entrance to Sam Wong Yung's fortune-teller's place.

Passing on, we next visited a hardware shop, where you could purchase various kinds of Chinese cutlery. Among other things that attracted my attention was a simple-looking Chinese fan, apparently folded up. On examining it I found that inside of the fan-case was a sharp knife or blade like a wide dagger. This could be carried in an unsuspecting manner into the midst of a company of men, and in a moment, if you had in your breast the wicked spirit of revenge, your enemy could be weltering in his life blood at your feet. It suggested all kinds of tragedies, and no doubt its invention had behind it some treacherous impulse. The writer ventured to purchase it, but he hastens to announce to his friends that his purposes are good and innocent. Though in the same category as the sword or dagger hidden in a walking-stick or a concealed weapon, this bloodthirsty knife will repose harmlessly in its fan-case like a sleeping babe in his cradle.

A Chinese boarding house next claimed our inspection. It was rather a forbidding place, but no doubt the Chinaman was well content with its accommodations. It was a long, rambling structure, and it seemed to me as if I were going through an underground passage in walking from room to room. The various halls were narrow, indeed so narrow that two persons meeting in them could not without difficulty pass each other. The beds, which brought a dollar a month, were one above another in tiers or recesses in the walls. Generally a curtain of a reddish hue depended in front of them. They reminded one of the berths in a ship or of the repositories of the dead in the Roman Catacombs. Two hundred and twenty-five persons were lodged in this dark, mysterious labyrinth. In another house there were five hundred and fifty people lodged in seventy-five rooms. Possibly the owners of tenement houses in our large cities, who crowd men and women into a narrow space and through unpitying agents reap a rich harvest regardless of the sufferings of their fellow-beings, have been taking lessons from the landlords of Chinatown. I said to myself, as I went to and fro through these narrow passages, dimly lighted with a lamp, and the lights were few and far between, if a fire should break out, at midnight, when all are wrapt in slumber, what a holocaust would be here! And whose would the sin and the shame be? There are good and ample fire-appliances for the protection of the city, but the poor Chinamen hemmed in, as in a dark prison-house, would surely be suffocated by smoke or be consumed in the flames. When the old theatre was burned down, twenty-five men, and probably more, perished, although there were means of escape from this building. I was told that the wood from which the largest hotel in Chinatown, its Palace hotel so to speak, was constructed in the early days, was brought around Cape Horn, and cost $350 per thousand feet. This was before saw-mills were erected in the forests among the foothills and on the slopes of the Sierras. The kitchen of the big boarding house was a novelty. It was nothing in any respect like the well-appointed kitchens of our hotels with their great ranges and open fire-places where meats may be roasted slowly on the turnspit. On one side of the kitchen there was a kind of stone-parapet about two feet and a half high, and on the top of this there were eight fire-places. As the Chinamen cook their own food there might be as many as eight men here at one time. I asked the guide if they ever quarreled. His answer was significant. "No! and it would be difficult to bring eight men of any other nationality together in such close proximity without differences arising and contentions taking place; but the Chinamen never trouble each other." There was only one man cooking at such a late hour as that in which we visited the kitchen, about half-past ten o'clock at night. He used charcoal, and as the coals were fanned the fire looked like that of a forge in a blacksmith's shop.

On our way to the Chinese Restaurant we stepped into a goldsmith's shop. There were a few customers present, and the proprietor waited on them with great diligence. At benches like writing desks, on which were tools of various descriptions, were seated some half a dozen workmen who were busily engaged. They never looked up while westood by and examined their work, which was of a high order. The filagree-work was beautiful and artistic. There were numerous personal ornaments, some of solid gold, others plaited. The bracelets which they were making might fittingly adorn the neck of a queen. I learned that these skilled men worked sixteen hours a day on moderate wages. Their work went into first-class Chinese bric-a-brac stores and into the jewelry stores of the merchants who supply the rich and cultured with their ornaments.

But it is time that we visit the restaurant. This is located in a stately building and is one of the first class. It overlooks the old Plaza, though you enter from the street one block west of the Plaza. You ascend broad stairs, and then you find yourself in a wide room or dining hall in two sections. Here are tables round and square, and here you are waited on by the sons of the Fiery Flying Dragon clad in well-made tunics, sometimes of silk material. As your eye studies the figure before you, the dress and the physiognomy, you do not fail to notice the long pigtail, the Chinaman's glory, as a woman's delight is her long hair. The tea, which is fragrant, is served to you out of dainty cups, China cups, an evidence that the tea-drinking of Americans and Europeans is derived from the Celestial Empire. The tea-plant is said, by a pretty legend, to have been formed from the eyelids of Buddha Dharma, which, in his generosity, he cut off for the benefit of men. If you wish for sweetmeats they will be served in a most tempting way. You can also have chicken, rice, and vegetables, and fruits, after the Chinese fashion. You can eat with your fingers if you like, or use knives and forks, or, if you desire to play the Chinaman, with the chop-sticks. In Chinatown the men and the women do not eat together. This is also the custom of China, and hence there is not what we look upon as an essential element of home-life - father and mother and children and guests, if there be such, gathered in a pleasant dining-room with the flow of edifying conversation and the exchange of courtesies. Confucius never talked when he ate, and his disciples affect his taciturnity at their meals. Though in scholastic times, in European institutions and in religious communities, men kept silence at their meals, yet the hours were enlivened by one who read for the edification of all. The interchange of thought, however, - the spoken word one with another, at the family table, is the better way. Silence may be golden, but speech is more golden if seasoned with wisdom; and even the pleasant jest and the *bon mot* have their office and exercise a salutary influence on character and conduct.

The food of Chinamen generally is very simple. Rice is the staple article of consumption. They like fruits and use them moderately. They eat things too, which would be most repulsive to the epicurean taste of an Anglo-Saxon. Even lizards and rats and young dogs they will not refuse. But these things are prepared in a manner to tempt the appetite. After you have partaken of your repast in the Chinese Restaurant, if you request it, tobacco pipes will be brought in, and your waiter will fill and light them for you and your friends. You can even, with a certain degree of caution, indulge in the opium pipe, the joy of the Chinaman. As you draw on this pipe and take long draughts you lapse into a strange state, all your ills seem to vanish, and you become indifferent to the world. The beggar in imagination becomes a millionaire, and for the time he feels that he is in the midst of courtly splendours. But, ah! When one awakes from his dream the pleasures are turned into ashes, and the glory fades as the fires of the pipe die. *Sic transit gloria mundi*! On the walls of the restaurant were various Chinese decorations. The inevitable lantern was in evidence. Here also were tablets with sentences in the language of the Celestials. But there was one thing that struck me forcibly as I examined the various objects in the rooms. In the rear half of the restaurant, on the north side of the room, stood a Chinese safe, somewhat in fashion like our ordinary American safe. It was not, however, secured with the combination lock with which we are all familiar. It shut like a cupboard, and had eight locks on a chain as it were. Every lock represented a man whose money or whose valuables were in the safe. Each of the eight men had a key for his own lock, different from all the other seven. When the safe is to be opened all the eight men must be present. Is this a comment on the honesty of the Chinaman? Is this indicative of their lack of confidence in each other? And yet as a house-servant the Chinaman is trusty and faithful and honest. He is also silent as to what transpires in his master's house and at his employer's table. The writer has conversed with people who have had Chinamen in their service, he has also visited the homes of gentlemen where only Chinese servants are employed in domestic work, and all bear testimony to their excellence and faithfulness and honesty.

No visit to Chinatown would be complete without an inspection of its theatre and a study of the audience. Here you see the Celestials *en masse*, you behold them in their amusements. Let us repair then to the Jackson Street Theatre. The building was once a hotel, now it is a place of pastime; and singularly under the same roof is a small Joss-House, - for the Chinaman couples his amusements with his religion. It rather reminds one of those buildings in Christian lands, which, while used for religious services, yet have kitchens and places for theatrical shows and amusements under the same roof. But the play has already begun. Indeed it began at six o'clock - and it is now nearly eleven P.M. It will, however, continue till midnight. This is the rule; for the Chinaman does nothing by halves, and he takes his amusement in a large quantity at a time. The theatre had galleries on three sides and these were packed with men and women as well as the main floor. There were altogether a thousand persons present, and it was indeed a strange sight to look into their faces, dressed alike as they were, and all seemingly looking alike. The women were seated in the west gallery on the right hand of the stage by themselves. This is an Eastern custom which Asiatic nations generally observe. Even in their religious assemblies the women sit apart. The custom arose primarily from the idea that woman is inferior to man. In the Jewish temple as well as in the synagogue, the sexes were separated. It is so to-day in most synagogues. Among the Mohammedans, too, woman is ruled out and is kept apart; and so strong is custom it even affected the Christian church in Oriental lands in the early days. You see a trace of it still in the East in church-arrangements.

A Chinese play takes a number of weeks or even months in which to complete it. It may be founded on domestic life or on some historic scene. Sometimes the history of a province of the Chinese Empire is the theme. The plays are mostly comedy. There are no grand tragedies like those of the old Greek poets. The Chinese have had no such writers as Sophocles or Euripides, no such creators of plays as Shakespeare, and they have no such actors as a Garrick or an Irving. We were invited to seats on the stage - which had no curtains, everything being done openly. In order to reach the stage the guide conducted us down the passageway or aisle through the midst of the audience. Then we ascended a platform at the end of the stage and went behind it into a long room where the actors were putting on costumes of a fantastic shape and painting their faces with bright coloured pigments. Some of them also put on masks that would frighten a person should he meet the wearers suddenly. The majority of the masks were caricatures of the human face and were comical in expression. We felt quite at home on the stage at once; for here, seated on either side with the actors in the midst of the company, were many of our friends lay and clerical, men and women, looking on in wonder at the strange performance. An orchestra of six or seven members was here on the back part of the stage - and the music! It consisted of the beating of drums, the sounding of gongs and other outlandish noises. Now and then above the din you could catch the sound of a clarionet and the feeble strains of a banjo. It was indeed pandemonium! Yet above all the noise and confusion you could hear the high pitched voices of the actors as they shouted and gesticulated. The audience, I noticed, was most attentive and decorous. They were evidently well pleased with the play; and what was quite remarkable they seemed to have neither ears nor eyes for their visitors. Of course they must have seen us, but with an indifference that almost bordered on contempt they paid no attention to us.

In the play one of the actors died on the stage, but the death had nothing of the tragic or heroic in it. After a brief interval he rose up and walked off amid the merriment of the audience.

Many Chinamen come here to spend their evening. The admission is fifty cents, which entitles one to a seat. As the play runs through six hours at a time, they feel that they get the worth of their money. They meet their friends there also; and although they are not very demonstrative towards each other, like the warm blooded races of Italy and Greece and Northern Europe and the United States, yet they are very happy in the presence of men of their own race and nation. The theatre is about the only place where they can meet on common ground, at least in large bodies, and then, as we have already intimated, the theatre is something more than a place of amusement in their eyes. Their forefathers liked such plays, and they believe that the spirits of the dead are in a certain sense present to share in the enjoyments of men in the body.

Only men and boys act on the Chinese stage. There are no women, though the female sex is personated. This has its advantages. Woman is kept out of harm; she is not subject to the indignities and temptations which beset her among other peoples who employ her services. Of course there are good and virtuous women on the stage - very many, I trust! But it will be admitted that the life of an actress is one of trial. She must of necessity be brought into intercourse with an element whose moral ideals are not the loftiest, and she must have unusual strength of character to preserve her integrity. She can do it! I believe that men and women can resist temptation in all spheres, in all vocations of life; I have great faith in humanity, especially when sustained by divine helps; but we must not subject the bow to too much tension lest it break. The personating of characters which have in them a spice of wickedness, the taking of the part in a play which represents the downfall of a virtuous person, the setting forth of the passions of love and hatred, must in time produce a powerful effect on the mind of a young woman, and there is danger that the neophyte on the stage will be contaminated with the base things of life before strength of character is developed. The Chinese are to be commended in this respect, whatever their motive in excluding their women from the stage. The reproduction of Greek plays, in some of our universities, where only men take the parts, shows what could be done among us on the stage, and successfully.

The Chinese actors whom I saw, exhibited a great deal of human nature in their acting. There was the full display of the human passions; and they entered into their work with zest as if it were real life. Some of the men in the audience were smoking cigars, others cigarettes. The Asiatic has a fondness for cigarettes. You see the men of the East smoking everywhere, whether in Syria, or Egypt, or Nubia, or Arabia. And is it not true that men are much the same the world over, in their pastimes and pursuits, their loves and their pleasures?

CHAPTER X

THE JOSS-HOUSE, CHINESE IMMIGRATION AND CHINESE THEOLOGY

In Chinatown - Conception of God - The Joss House - Chinese Mottoes - The Joss a Chinaman - Greek and Egyptian Ideas of God - Different Types of Madonnas - Chinese Worship and Machine Prayers - The Joss-House and the Christian Church - Chinese Immigration - Chinamen in the United States - A Plague Spot - Fire Crackers and Incense Sticks - The Lion and the Hen - The Man with Tears of Blood - Filial Piety - The Joss - Origin of the World - Creation of Man - Spirits of the Dead - Ancestral Rites - The Chinese Emperor - What Might Have Been - The Hand of God.

Our study of Chinatown and the civilisation of the country of the Yellow Dragon, as seen in the City of the Golden Gate, has thus far brought us in contact with the social and business life of the Chinese and their amusements; but we are now to visit one of their temples of worship, the Joss-House. And here the real man will be revealed; for it is in religious services and ceremonies and beliefs that we get a true knowledge of a race or a nation. The conception of God which you have is the key to your character. If your views of Deity are low and ignoble you will not achieve any greatness in the world; but if on the other hand you invest the Being Whom you worship with noble attributes and look upon Him as just and holy, a God of mercy and judgment, your breast will be animated with grand thoughts and lofty ideals will impel you to the performance of heroic deeds. The word Joss, which we use for a Chinese idol or god, seems to be derived from the Portugese, Dios, or rather it is the Pidgin English of Dios. A Joss-House then is a Chinese idol or god-house. We are now standing before such a place of worship. This is on the corner of Kearney and Pine Streets, and is built of brick, and as we look up we see that it is three stories high. There is a marble slab over the entrance with an inscription which tells us that this building is the Sze-Yap Asylum. Let us enter. The lower story, we find, is given up to business of one kind or another connected with the Sze-Yap Immigration Society. This, we note, is richly adorned with valuable tapestries and silken hangings, and the rich colours attract the eye at once. If you wish to sit down you can, and enjoy the novelty of the scene. For here are easy chairs which invite you to rest. In your inspection of the place you venture to peer into the room back of this, and you perceive at once that there is the lounging place of the establishment. You see men on couches perfectly at ease and undisturbed by your presence, smoking cigarettes or opium, the Chinaman's delight. If you desire to penetrate further into the building you will come to the kitchen where the dainty dishes of the Chinese are cooked; but you retreat and ascend a staircase in the southeast corner of the first room, and soon you are in the Joss-House proper. This second story is devoted exclusively to religious purposes. The room to which you are now introduced is about thirty feet square, and as you look around you perceive the hangings on the walls and the rich decorations of the ceiling. Here are placards on the walls, which, your guide will tell you, if you are not conversant with the Chinese tongue, bear on them sentences from the writings of Confucius, Mencius, and others, with exhortations to do nothing against integrity or virtue, to venerate ancestors and to be careful not to injure one's reputation in the eyes of Americans; - all of which is most excellent advice, and worthy of the attention of men everywhere. You then cast your eyes on the gilded spears, and standards and battle-axes standing in the corners of the Temple, and as you look up you almost covet the great Chinese lanterns suspended from the ceiling. Your eyes are finally directed to the altar, near which, and on it, are flowers artificial and natural. At the rear in a kind of a niche in the Joss or god. The figure of this deity was like a noble Chinaman, well-dressed, with a moustache, and having in his eyes a far-away expression. He wore a tufted crown, which made him look somewhat war-like. It is but natural that this Joss should be a blind man. The Greek gods and goddesses have Greek countenances. The idolatrous nations fashion their deities after their own likeness. And what are these but deified human beings? It is so in Greek and Roman mythology. The Egyptian Osiris is an Egyptian. It is true that some of the ancients outside of Hebrew Revelation had a better conception of God than others. Even in Egypt where birds and beasts and creeping things received divine honors there were scholars and poets who had an exalted idea of the Deity, as witness the Poems of Pentaur. This is true also of some of the Greek Poets who had a deep insight into divine things. It is not a little interesting to note also that artists of different nations paint the Madonna after the style of their own women. Very few of the pictures in the great art galleries are after the style of face which you see in the Orient. Hence there are Dutch Madonnas, and Italian and French and English types. There were no worshippers in the Joss-House at the hour when I visited it. Worship is not a prominent feature of Chinese religious life. The good Chinaman comes once a year at least, perhaps oftener, and burns a bit of perforated paper before his Joss, in order to show that he is not forgetful of his deity. This bit of paper is about six inches long and two inches wide. He also puts printed or written papers in a machine which is run like a clock. Well, this is an easy way to say prayers. And are there not many prayers offered, not merely by Chinamen, that are machine prayers, soulless, heartless, meaningless, and faithless, and which bring no answer? But how simple, how beautiful, how sublime, the golden Prayer which the Divine Master taught His disciples! Lord, teach us how to pray. If the noble Liturgy of the Church is properly rendered, - for it is the expansion of the Lord's Prayer, - there will be no machine-praying, and the answer to prayer will be rich and abundant. The contrast between the worship of the Joss and the worship of the true God in a Christian Church is striking and affords reflection. The former is of the earth earthy, the latter transports the devout worshipper to the throne of the Most High. There is no fear that the religion of the Joss-House will ever usurp the religion of the Christian altar. Men have expressed the fear that if the Chinese came in overwhelming numbers to America they would endanger the Christian faith by their idolatry. But would this be true? Has Christianity anything to dread? What impression has the Joss-House made all these years on the life of San Francisco outside of Chinatown? None whatever, except to make the reflecting man value the Christian faith with its elevating influences and its blessed hopes all the more.

It is a mistake then to exclude Chinamen from our shores on the ground that they will do harm to Christianity. On the contrary the Church will do them good. The Gospel is the leaven which will be the salvation of heathen men. Did it not go forth into the Gentile world on its glorious mission, and did it not convert many nations in the first ages? Has it lost its potency to-day? No! It is as powerful as ever to win men from their idols and their evil lives. The question of Chinese immigration is a large one. It has its social and its political aspects. It is found all along the Pacific coast that Chinamen make good and faithful servants. The outcry against them as competing with white laborers and artisans is more the result of political agitation for political purposes than good judgment. Where they have been displaced on farms, in mills, in warehouses, in domestic life, white men and women have not been found to take their places and do the work which they can do so well. Under the Geary Act immigration has been restricted and the numbers of the Chinese in the United States have been gradually decreasing. In the year 1854 there were only 3,000 Chinese in the City of San Francisco; but even then there was agitation against them. It was Governor Bigler who called them "coolies," and this term they repudiated with the same abhorrence which the negro or black man has for the term "nigger." They kept on increasing, however, until in 1875 there were in the whole State of California 130,000. Of this number 30,000 were in San Francisco. To-day there are only about 46,000 in California and there are not more than thirty thousand of these in the City of San Francisco. There are only 110,000 Chinese altogether in the United States proper. Even the most ardent exclusionist can see from this that there is nothing to dread as to an overwhelming influx that will threaten the integrity and existence of our civilisation. The labour-question and the race-question and the international question, aroused by the presence of the Chinese within our borders, will from time to time cause agitation and provoke discussion and heated debate and evoke oratory of one kind or another; but the question which should be uppermost in the minds of wise statesmen is how shall they be assimilated to our life? How shall we make them Christians? The answer will be the best solution of the whole matter, if it has in mind the spiritual interests of the Chinaman and of all other heathen on our shores. There is indeed a plague spot in Chinatown, the social fester, which can and ought to be removed. But this is true of American San Francisco as well as of Chinatown. What, we may ask, are the men and women of as beautiful a city as ever sat on Bay or Lake or Sea-Shore or River, doing for its purgation, for its release from moral defilement and "garments spotted with the flesh?" This indeed is one of the searching questions to be asked of any other City, such as New York, Chicago, St. Louis, London, Paris, Cairo, Constantinople, as well as San Francisco. Among the other noticeable things in the Joss-House were two immense lanterns, as much for ornament as for utility. Then I saw a big drum and a bell, used in some of the processions of the Temple; for the Chinese take special delight in noises, indeed the more noise the better satisfied they are. During my visit some of the Joss-House attendants were shooting off fire crackers; and I was told that this was an acceptable offering to the Chinese god. One who was selling small, slender incense sticks, said that you could burn them to drive away the devil, an excellent purpose certainly. He also said they were good to keep moths away. Doubtless in the Chinese mind there is a connection between moths and evil spirits; but you smile at all such puerilities. They belong to the childhood of the world and not to the beginning of the twentieth century. Among other creatures which they venerate are chickens and lions. They invest the lion with divine attributes on account of his majesty and power. But the chicken? Well, it is a gentle creature. It is the embodiment of motherhood and it speaks of care, not only to the Chinaman's understanding, but to ours also. The Divine Teacher, greater than Confucius, said: "How often would I have gathered thy children together as a hen gathereth her chickens under her wings!" Will China, now waking out of the sleep of centuries, allow Him to gather her children together under the wings of His Cross? "And ye would not." Oh, what pathos in these few words! But doubtless they will. Many during the war of the Boxers were "gathered" unto Him, emulating the zeal and courage and faith of the martyrs of the early days of the Church. As the hen is sacred in the eyes of the Chinaman, sacred as the peacock to Juno or the ibis to the Egyptians, they swear by her head, and an oath thus taken may not be broken.

One of the images which I saw in the Joss-House was pointed out as the God of the Door; and how suggestive this title and this office! Another figure, on the right side of the altar, which attracted my attention particularly was that of Toi Sin. He was dressed somewhat like a mandarin, and his head was bared, while tears as of blood were on his cheeks. He lived some three hundred years after the Advent of Christ; and owing to his disobedience to his parents, for which he was punished in his conscience, and otherwise, he grieved himself to death and wept tears of blood. His image, I was told, is placed in all Temples as a warning to children. It is a forceful lesson, and it is a timely warning. The one thing that is characteristic of a Chinaman is his filial piety. This filial piety was admired in all ages. It was inculcated in the old Hebrew Law and enforced with weighty considerations. It was a virtue among the Greeks as well as other peoples of the Gentile world; and I wonder not that when the heroes who captured Troy saw Aeneas carrying his aged father Anchises on his shoulders and leading his son, the puer Ascanius, by the hand, out of the burning city, they cheered him and allowed him to escape with his precious burden. A Chinaman is taught by precept and example to venerate his parents and to give them divine honors after death. Should a Chinese child be disobedient he would be punished severely by the bamboo or other instrument, and he would bring on himself the wrath of all his family. This strong sense of filial piety has done more for the stability and perpetuity of the Chinese Empire than ought else. It is a great element of strength and it leads to respect for customs and to the observance of maxims. Especially are burial places held in sacred esteem, and as they contain the ashes of the fathers they must not be disturbed or desecrated. In this respect we might emulate the Chinese, for they are a perfect illustration of the old precept, "Honour thy father and thy mother," which, in a busy, independent age, there is danger of forgetting. But we look with no little interest on the Joss above the altar, the Chinese god. His name is Kwan Rung, and I am informed that he was born about two hundred years after the beginning of the Christian era. Such is the person who is worshipped here. That he may not be hungry food is placed before him at times, and also water to drink. It is a poor, weak human god after all, a dying, dead man. How different the Creator of the ends of the earth, Who fainteth not neither is weary! The Chinese have no conception of the true God. They cannot conceive of the beauty and power and compassion of Jesus Christ until they are brought into the light of the Gospel. But what is Chinese theology? What do they teach about the origin of the world and man and his destiny. The scholars tell us that the world was formed by the duel powers Yang and Yin, who were in turn influenced by their own creations. First the heavens were brought into being, then the earth. From the co-operation of Yang and Yin the four seasons were produced, and the seasons gave birth to the fruits and flowers of the earth. The dual principles also brought forth fire and water, and the sun and moon and stars were originated. The idea of a Creator in the Biblical sense is far removed from the Chinese mind. Their first man, named Pwanku, after his appearance, was set to work to mould the Chaos out of which he was born. He had also to chisel out the earth which was to be his abode. Behind him through the clefts made by his chisel and mallet are sun and moon and stars, and at his right hand, as companions, may be seen the Dragon, the Tortoise and the Phoenix as well as the Unicorn. His labours extend over a period of eighteen thousand years. He grew in stature at the rate of six feet every day, and when his work was finished he died. The mountains were formed from his head, his breath produced the wind, and the moisture of his lips the clouds. His voice is the thunder, his limbs are the four poles, his veins the rivers, his sinews the wave-like motions of the earth, his flesh the fields, his beard the stars, his skin and hair herbs and trees, his teeth bones, his marrow metals, rocks and precious stones, his sweat rain, and the insects clinging to his body become men and women. Ah, how applicable the memorable line of Horace!

Parturiunt montes, nascetur ridiculus mus.

In regard to the spirits of the dead the Chinese believe that they linger still in the places which were their homes while alive on earth, and that they can be moved to pleasure or pain by what they see or hear. These spirits of the departed are delighted with offerings rendered to them and take umbrage at neglect. Believing also that the spirits can help or injure men they pray to them and make offerings to them. From this we can understand the meaning and object of ancestral rites. In these rites they honour and assist the dead as if they were alive still. Food, clothing and money are offered, as they believe they eat and drink and have need of the things of this life. Even theatrical exhibitions and musical entertainments are provided on the presumption that they are gratified with what pleased them while in the body. Now as all past generations are to be provided for, the Chinese Pantheon contains myriads of beings to be worshipped. But think, what a burden it becomes to the poor man who tries conscientiously to do his duty to the departed!

Now this ancestral worship leads to the deduction that it is an unfilial thing not to marry and beget sons by whom the line of descendants may be continued. Otherwise the line would cease, and the spirits would have none to care for them or worship them.

The Chinese view of rulers or Kings is also striking. According to the belief prevalent regarding government, Heaven and Earth were without speech. These created man who should represent them. This man is none other than the Emperor their vicegerent. He is constituted ruler over all people. This accounts for three things; first, the superiority which the Chinese emperors assume over the kings and rulers of other countries; secondly, for the long-lived empire of

China, it being rebellion against Heaven to lift up one's self against the Emperor; and in the third place it explains to us why divine honours are paid to him. He is a sacred person. He is in a certain sense a god. The view is similar to that entertained by the Roman Emperors, who, in inscriptions and on coins employed the term Deus, and at times exacted divine honours. As we turn from the Joss-House and walk away from this bit of heathendom in the heart of an active, stirring, prosperous, great American city with its Christian civilisation and its Christian Churches and its Christian homes, we cannot but ask ourselves what would have been the history of the Pacific States, of California with its nearly eight hundred miles of coast, if the Chinese had settled here centuries ago? If they had been navigators and colonizers like the Phoenicians of old, like the Greeks and Romans, if they had had a Columbus, a Balboa, a Cabrillo, a Drake, the whole history of the country west of the Rocky Mountains might have been totally different. Millions of Chinamen instead of thousands might now be in possession of that great region of our land, and great cities like Canton and Fuchau, Pekin and Tientsin, might rise up on the view instead of San Diego and Los Angeles, Sacramento and San Francisco, with their idolatry and peculiar life and customs. Another question may be asked here by way of speculation. What would have been the effect of Chinese occupation of the Pacific coast on the Indians of all the region west of the Rocky Mountains? Would the followers of Confucius have incorporated them into their nationality, supplanted them, or caused them to vanish out of sight? What problems these for the ethnologist! Doubtless there would have been intermarriages of the races with new generations of commingled blood. And what would have been the result of this? There is a story which I have read somewhere, that long years ago a Chinese junk was driven by the winds to the shores of California, and that a Chinese merchant on board took an Indian maiden to wife and bore her home to the Flowery Kingdom, and that from this marriage was descended the famous statesman Li Hung Chang. But whatever the fortunes of the Indians, or the Chinese in their appropriation of the Pacific coast, it would not have been so advantageous to civilisation, to the progress of humanity. It would have been loss, and a hindrance to the Anglo-Saxon race destined now to rule the world and to break down every barrier and to set up the standard of the Cross everywhere for the glory of the true God. His hand is apparent in it all. He directs the great movements of history for the welfare of mankind, and He controls the destinies of nations for the advancement of His Kingdom!

CHAPTER XI

THE GENERAL CONVENTION OF 1901

First Services - Drake's Chaplain - Flavel Scott Mines - Bishop Kip - Growth of the Church in California - The General Convention in San Francisco - A Western Sermon - Personnel of the Convention - Distinguished Names - Subjects Debated - Missions of the Church - Apportionment Plan - The Woman's Auxiliary - The United Offering - Missionary Meeting in Mechanics' Pavilion - College Reunions - Zealous Men - A Dramatic Scene - Closing Service - Object Lesson - A Revelation to California - Examples of the Church's Training - Mrs. Twing - John I. Thompson - Golden Gate of Paradise.

As we turn away from Chinatown, with its Oriental customs and its peculiar life and its religion, we naturally give ourselves up to reflection on the mission and character of the Christian Church. While we recognise the good that is done by "all who profess and call themselves Christians," and thank God for every good work done in the name and for the sake of Jesus Christ, we may more especially consider the development of the Episcopal Church, pure and Apostolic in its origin, on the Pacific coast. We must ever keep in mind the services held in this region as far back as the year 1579, by Chaplain Francis Fletcher, under

Admiral Drake, when the old Prayer Book of the Church of England was used on the shores of the Golden Gate, a fact commemorated, as we have already noted in a previous chapter, by the Prayer Book Cross erected by the late George W. Childs, of Philadelphia, in Golden Gate Park. This was prophetic of bright days to come. Time would roll on and bring its marvellous changes, but the truth of God would remain the same, and the Church would still flourish and the liturgy of our forefathers would hold its place in the affections of the people of all ranks, as at this day. Drake and Fletcher could hardly have realised, however, that the good seed which they then sowed, though it might remain hidden from view for many generations, would in time spring-up and yield a glorious harvest. We are not unmindful, of course, of the labours and teachings of the Franciscans among the California Indians; but when this order of things passed away and the Anglo-Saxon succeeded the Spaniard and the Mexican, it was but natural that the old Church which had made Great Britain what it was and is, aye, and moulded our civilisation on this continent, should seek a foothold in the beautiful lands by the Pacific and on the slopes of the Sierras. Many of the Church's sons were among the thousands who sought California in quest of gold, and these Argonauts she would follow whithersoever they went. They must not be left alone to wrestle with the temptations which would beset them far away from home and the hallowing influences of sacred institutions and religious services. Hence it is that we behold that zealous missionary of the Church, the Rev. Flavel Scott Mines, going forth to seek out Christ's sheep in San Francisco and elsewhere, and to gather them into the fold of the Good Shepherd. His history is most interesting and instructive. He was the son of Rev.

John Mines, D.D., a Presbyterian clergyman of Virginia, and was born in Leesburg, Va., on the 31st of December, 1811. In 1830 he was graduated from Princeton Theological Seminary, and soon after he became pastor of the Laight Street Presbyterian Church, New York city, where he served with distinction until he resigned his charge in 1841. In 1842 he took orders in the Church, of which to the day of his death he was a loyal son. Reasons for becoming a churchman and the motives which impelled him are set forth in a striking and graphic manner in his monumental book, "A Presbyterian Clergyman Looking For the Church," a work of marked ability and of great utility. It had a large sale in his day, and it is still sought after as a book of permanent value. It is a strong plea for Apostolic Order and Liturgical Worship, and it is safe to say that it has been instrumental in leading many an inquirer into the "old paths" and the Faith as "once delivered to the Saints." The Rev. Mr. Mines, after his ordination, became assistant minister in St. George's Church, New York city, under Rev. Dr. James Milnor. From here he went to the Danish West Indies and became Rector of St. Paul's Parish, Fredericksted, St. Croix, about forty miles square and embracing almost half of the island. Owing to failing health he returned, after many arduous labours, to the United States, and became Rector of St. Luke's Church, Rossville, Staten Island. He went finally to San Francisco, where he preached for the first time on July 8th, 1849, in the midst of the gold excitement, and on July 22nd of this same year, became the founder of Trinity Parish, where his honoured name is still held in grateful remembrance, not merely by some of the twenty-two original members, who still live, but by their children and grandchildren. The first Trinity Church was located on the northeast corner of Post and Powell Streets. It was a modest building, which, in 1867, gave place to an edifice, Gothic in design, costing $85,000. A few years ago the present Trinity Church was erected on the northeast corner of Bush and Gough Streets, with ample grounds for parish buildings. This sacred edifice is one of the finest and largest churches on the Pacific coast, and is a combination of Spanish and Byzantine styles of architecture. It was designed by A. Paige Brown, who was the architect of the California building at the Columbian Exposition, in Chicago, and also of the new Bethesda Church, Saratoga Springs, N.Y. I have thus dwelt with particularity on the Rev. Flavel Scott Mines's life and work, because Trinity Parish is the mother of all the other Parishes in California, and because here in this new edifice, where there is a tablet to his memory, and where he is buried, the General Convention was held in 1901, a council of the Church which will ever be memorable. It is well also to rescue from oblivion the memory of a man who laid the foundations of the Church in California on the enduring principles of the ancient creeds. May we not learn also from the facts of his life, which show how faithful and accomplished he was, that the men who are to be heralds of the Cross in new fields are to be the ablest and the best equipped that the Church can furnish? Other early missionaries of the Church who may be named here are the Rev. Dr. Ver Mehr, who arrived in San Francisco in September, 1849, and in 1850 founded Grace Parish; and Rev. John Morgan, who organised Christ Church Parish in 1853; and Rev. Dr. Christopher B. Wyatt, who succeeded Mines in Trinity Church. There is another also whose name is interwoven in the history of the Church's mission in California. It is that of Right Rev. William Ingraham Kip, D.D., LL.D., who was consecrated first Bishop of

California, October 28, 1853. Few, if any, of his day, were better fitted in scholarship, zeal, and other gifts and qualifications for his work than he, who is the famous author of "The Double Witness of the Church," a book which has largely moulded the faith and practice of the churchmen of this generation. Bishop Kip's immortal work and Mines's incomparable volume deserve to be ranked together, and though they differ widely in their manner of presenting the Old Faith, yet are they one in purpose. Is it not a little singular, or is it not rather a happy coincidence, that the two foremost pioneers of the Church's work in California should thus be the authors of works which are fit to take rank with the Apologiai of the early Christian writers or the "Apologia pro Ecclesia Anglicana" of Bishop Jewell?

Mines went to his rest in 1852, just in the prime of life, while Kip was spared to the Church until 1893, witnessing its great increase and reaping the abundant harvest from that early sowing. The growth is seen to-day in the three dioceses in the State. California, the parent diocese, with San Francisco as its chief city, Right Rev. William Ford Nichols, D.D., Bishop, has its eighty-one clergymen, with its eighty-six parishes and missions, and 8,585 communicants. Los Angeles, Right Rev. Joseph Horsfall Johnson, D.D., Bishop, has its forty-nine clergy, with its fifty-six parishes and missions, and 4,577 communicants; while Sacramento, Right Rev. William Hall Moreland, D.D., Bishop, has thirty-four clergymen with seventy parishes and missions, and a list of 2,556 communicants. All this, however, is not the full evidence of the strength of the Church on the Pacific coast. There are the church schools and hospitals and other agencies for good, and there are the blessed influences which the Church, with her stability and order and work, is exerting among the people. The results arising from the presence of the members of the General Convention will be gratifying. Everywhere throughout the State of California this august body was hailed with a glad welcome, and San Francisco and her suburban towns did everything possible to make churchmen feel at home. The attendance at services was large, and a deep and an abiding interest was enkindled. It was said by the press and by leading citizens, that while many bodies had met in San Francisco from all parts of the land, none had ever surpassed in standard that of the Convention or even equalled it in dignity, scholarship, eloquence and other noted characteristics. The newspapers of the city, such as the *Daily Call* and the *Chronicle*, gave up large space to the services, debates and other features of the Convention, and they were always complimentary in their comments on individuals as well as on receptions and sermons and addresses. The keynote of the Convention was struck by the Right Rev. Benjamin Wistar Morris, D.D., Bishop of Oregon, in his sermon based on St. Luke, chapter v, verse 4: - "Now when He had left speaking, He said unto Simon, Launch out into the deep, and let down your nets for a draught." The discourse was in every sense what the venerable prelate had said it would be, a "Western" one, and it was a powerful plea setting forth the urgent necessity of extending and supporting the Church in her missionary efforts in the Pacific coast States.

The attendance of members in the House of Deputies was unusually large, and while some familiar faces were missed, like Dean Hoffman, of the General Theological Seminary; Rev. Dr. Morgan Dix, of Trinity Parish, New York; Rev. Dr. Edward A. Renouf, of Keene, N.H.; Rev. Dr. W.W. Battershall, of Albany,

N.Y.; Mr. Spencer Trask, of Yaddo, Saratoga Springs, N.Y.; Mr. Louis Hasbrouck, of Ogdensburgh, N.Y.; Mr. G.P. Keese, of Cooperstown, N.Y.; and Judge Robert Earl, of Herkimer, N.Y., yet the personnel of the Convention was up to the usual standard. The new deputies, clerical and lay, felt at home at once, and some of them made good reputations for themselves in debate and in committee-work. It would seem invidious, perhaps, to single out any one deputy more than another, when all excelled, yet the names of some of the representative clergymen and laymen of the Church may justly be mentioned, as for example, Rev. Dr. John S. Lindsay, of Boston, Mass., the distinguished and well-balanced President of the House; Rev. Dr. Arthur Lawrence, of Stockbridge, Mass.; Rev. Dr. Reese F. Alsop, of Brooklyn, N.Y.; Rev. Dr. J. Houston Eccleston, of Baltimore, Md.; Rev. Dr. Samuel D. McConnell, of Brooklyn, N.Y.; Rev. Dr. J.S. Hodges, of Baltimore, Md.; Rev. Dr. George Hodges, of Cambridge, Mass.; Rev. Dr. Cameron Mann, of Kansas City, Mo.; Rev. Dr. James W. Ashton, of Olean, N.Y.; Rev. Dr. Robert J. Nevin, of Rome, Italy; Rev. Dr. John Fulton, of *The Church Standard*, Philadelphia, Pa.; Rev. Dr. William B, Bodine, of Philadelphia, Pa.; Rev. Dr. Charles S. Olmstead, of Bala, Pa.; Rev. Dr. George McClellan Fiske, of Providence, R.I.; Rev. Dr. Edgar A. Enos, of Troy, N.Y.; Rev. Dr. J. Lewis Parks and Rev. Dr. William M. Grosvenor of New York; Rev. Dr. R.M. Kirby, of Potsdam, N.Y.; Rev. Dr. John H. Egar, of Rome, N.Y.; Rev. Dr. George D. Silliman, of Stockport, N.Y.; Rev. Dr. John Brainard, of Auburn, N.Y.; Rev. Dr. H. Martyn Hart, of Denver, Col.; Rev. Dr. Edwin S. Lines, of New Haven, Conn; Rev. Dr. Daniel C. Roberts, of Concord, N.H.; Rev. Dr. Alfred B. Baker, of Princeton, N.J.; Rev. George S. Bennitt, of Jersey City, N.J.; Rev. Dr. J. Isham Bliss, of Burlington, Vt.; Rev. John Henry Hopkins, of Chicago, Ill.; Rev. Dr. Campbell Fair, of Omaha, Neb.; Rev. John Williams, of Omaha, Neb.; Rev. Dr. Frederick W. Clampett, of San Francisco, Cal; Rev. R.G. Foute, of San Francisco, Cal.; Rev. Dr. Angus Crawford, of Alexandria Seminary, Va.; Rev. Dr. Randolph H. McKim, of Washington, D.C.; Rev. Dr. Frederick P. Davenport, of Memphis, Tenn.; Rev. Dr. Alex. Mackay-Smith, of Washington, D.C.; Rev. Henry B. Restarick, of San Diego, Cal.; Rev. B.W.R. Tayler, of Los Angeles, Cal.; Rev. Dr. David H. Greer, of New York; Rev. Dr. William R. Huntington, of New York; Rev. Dr. Beverly D. Tucker, of Norfolk, Va.; Rev. Dr. Carl E. Grammer, of Norfolk, Va.; Rev. Dr. William T. Manning, of Nashville, Tenn.; Rev. Frederick A. De Rosset, of Cairo, Ill.; Rev. Richard P. Williams, of Washington, D.C.; Rev. Dr. Henry W. Nelson, of Geneva, N.Y.; Rev. Dr. John Kershaw, of Charleston, S.C.; Rev. Dr. Herman C. Duncan, of Alexandria, La.; Rev. Dr. John K. Mason, of Louisville, Ky.; Rev. Dr. Walter R. Gardner, of Algoma, Wis.; Rev. Dr. George C. Hall, of Wilmington, Del; Rev. J.L. McKim, of Milford, Del.; Rev. Dr. Henry L. Jones, of Wilkesbarre, Pa.; Rev. Dr. George C. Foley, of Williamsport, Pa.; Rev. Dr. Storrs O. Seymour, of Litchfield, Conn.; Rev. Dr. Charles E. Craik, of Louisville, Ky.; Rev. C.S. Leffingwell, of Bar Harbour, Me.; Rev. Dr. Rufus W. Clark, of Detroit, Mich.; Rev. Dr. Lucius Waterman, of Claremont, N.H.; Rev. Dr. Henry H. Oberly, of Elizabeth, N.J.; Rev. Julian E. Ingle, of Henderson, N.C.; Rev. Dr. Charles L. Hutchins, of Concord, Mass., the efficient Secretary, always patient and courteous; Rev. Dr. Henry Anstice, of Philadelphia, Pa.; Rev. Edward W. Worthington, of Cleveland, Ohio, and Rev. William C.

Prout, of Herkimer, N.Y., Assistant Secretaries; Mr. George M. Darrow, of Murfreesboro, Tenn.; Dr. William Seward Webb, of Shelburne, Vt.; Mr. Henry E. Pellew, of Washington, D.C.; Mr. Linden H. Morehouse, of Milwaukee, Wis., of *The Young Churchman* Co.; Judge James M. Woolworth, of Omaha, Neb.; Mr. Burton Mansfield, of New Haven, Conn.; Hon. Cortlandt Parker, of Newark, N.J.; Judge Charles Andrews, of Syracuse, N.Y.; Mr. John I. Thompson, of Troy, N.Y.; Mr. Leslie Pell-Clarke, of Springfield Centre, N.Y.; Hon. George R. Fairbanks, of Fernandina, Fla.; Judge L. Bradford Prince, of Santa Fe, N.M.; Hon. Francis A. Lewis, of Philadelphia, Pa.; Hon. Francis L. Stetson, of New York; Mr. George C. Thomas, of Philadelphia, Pa., Treasurer of the Board of Missions; Hon. W. Bayard Cutting, of New York; Judge John H. Stiness, of Providence, R.I.; Hon. Joseph Packard, of Baltimore, Md.; Hon. Charles G. Saunders, of Lawrence, Mass.; Hon. Arthur J.C. Sowdon, and Hon. Robert Treat Paine, of Boston, Mass; Mr. William B. Hooper, of San Francisco; Mr. Henry P. Baldwin, of Detroit, Mich.; Mr. Francis J. McMaster, of St. Louis, Mo.; Mr. William H. Lightner, of St. Paul, Minn.; Mr. Richard H. Battle, of Raleigh, N.C.; Hon. G.S. Gadsden, of Charleston, S.C.; Mr. George Truesdell, of Washington, D.C.; Mr. George M. Marshall, of Salt Lake City, Utah; and Mr. Joseph Wilmer, of Alexandria Seminary, Va. There is one other name which must not be omitted, that of Mr. J. Pierpont Morgan, of New York city, who, notwithstanding his vast business interests, was in his seat from the opening of the Convention until the closing session, watching all the debates and deliberations with the deepest interest, and serving on various important committees. Many of the members of the Convention, too, were deeply indebted to him for a gracious hospitality dispensed by him in his magnificent temporary home on California Avenue.

To name the Bishops who in one way and another made their presence felt in their own House, in the Board of Missions and elsewhere, at meetings and in services, it would be necessary to speak of all who were in attendance on the Convention. Those who were specially active, however, were Bishop William Croswell Doane, of Albany; Bishop Henry Codman Potter, of New York; Bishop Daniel Sylvester Tuttle, of Missouri; Bishop Benjamin Wistar Morris, of Oregon; Bishop Thomas Underwood Dudley, of Kentucky; Bishop Ozi William Whitaker, of Pennsylvania; Bishop Cortlandt Whitehead, of Pittsburg; Bishop John Scarborough, of New Jersey; Bishop George Franklin Seymour, of Springfield; Bishop William David Walker, of Western New York; Bishop Leighton Coleman, of Delaware; Bishop Samuel David Ferguson, of Cape Palmas; Bishop Ellison Capers, of South Carolina; Bishop Theodore Nevin Morrison, of Iowa; Bishop Lewis William Burton, of Lexington; Bishop Sidney Catlin Partridge, of Kyoto; Bishop Peter Trimble Rowe, of Alaska; Bishop William Frederick Taylor, of Quincy; Bishop William Crane Gray, of Southern Florida; Bishop Ethelbert Talbot, of Central Pennsylvania; Bishop James Steptoe Johnston, of Western Texas; Bishop Anson Rogers Graves, of Laramie; Bishop Edward Robert Atwill, of West Missouri; Bishop William N. McVickar, of Rhode Island; Bishop William Lawrence, of Massachusetts; Bishop Arthur C.A. Hall, of Vermont; Bishop William Andrew Leonard, of Ohio; Bishop James Dow Morrison, of Duluth; Bishop Henry Yates Satterlee, of Washington; Bishop Charles C. Grafton, of Fond du Lac; Bishop Abiel Leonard, of

Salt Lake; Bishop Isaac Lea Nicholson, of Milwaukee; Bishop Cleland Kinlock Nelson, of Georgia, and Bishop Thomas F. Gailor, of Tennessee. It is needless to say that Right Rev. Dr. William Ford Nichols, of California, who was the host of the Convention, was prominent in all gatherings, and that his guiding hand was seen in all the admirable arrangements made for meetings and services. He was ably seconded by Bishop Johnson, of Los Angeles, and Bishop Moreland, of Sacramento. Some faces were sadly missed, as for example, Bishop Niles, of New Hampshire; Bishop Huntington, of Central New York; Bishop Worthington, of Nebraska; Bishop Spaulding, of Colorado; and the Presiding Bishop, Right Rev. Thomas March Clark, of Rhode Island. The Secretary of the House of Bishops, Rev. Dr. Samuel Hart, of Middletown, Conn., was a conspicuous figure in the Convention, and he and his assistants, Rev. Dr. George F. Nelson, of New York, and Rev. Thomas J. Packard, of Washington, were often seen in the House of Deputies, bearing official messages.

In addition to the regular business of the Convention, there were discussions of a high order on such matters as Amendments to the Constitution, the enactment of New Canons, Admission of New Dioceses, Marriage and Divorce, and Marginal Readings in the Bible. The Report of the Commission on Marginal Readings was finally adopted, with some modifications, after an animated debate, to the great satisfaction of many who felt the need of such a help in reading the Holy Scriptures. At times the speakers, both lay and clerical, rose to heights of fervid oratory, and it was an education to listen to men who were thoroughly versed in the themes which they handled. The Missions of the Church were not neglected in the midst of the exciting debates of the Convention, and an important step was taken when the Board resolved to adopt the Apportionment Plan, by which each diocese and missionary jurisdiction would be called on to raise a definite sum of money. This, it was felt, would relieve the Board from the burden of indebtedness, and would enable the Church to originate new work. No more earnest advocates of this plan could be found in the meetings of the two Houses of Convention as the Board of Missions, than in Bishop Brewer of Montana and Mr. George C. Thomas, the Treasurer. Their words were forcible and their manner magnetic. Bishop Doane's eloquent advocacy of the measure also led to happy results.

In this chapter on the Triennial Council of the Church held in San Francisco, we must not omit to make mention of the United Offering of the Woman's Auxiliary to the Board of Missions. The women of the Church specially devoted to its missionary work had been gradually increasing their forces and activities and offerings. When they last met, in the city of Washington, D.C., three years before, they presented the goodly sum of $83,000; but now in San Francisco they were to surpass their previous efforts. They were to show forth the fruits of more earnest labours and richer giving. They established their headquarters at 1609 Sutter street, in a commodious dwelling house, not far from Trinity Church, where the Convention was in session. Here various rooms were fitted up with handiwork and other products of missionary labour from the numerous fields where the Church, in obedience to her Lord's command, is engaged in sowing beside all waters; and no one could walk through these artistic chambers adorned with the work of the Indians of Alaska and the dwellers of the South Seas, the converts of India, of China and Japan, as well as Mexico and other regions, without being filled with admiration. Various dioceses also of the Church exhibited pictures of sacred edifices showing different styles of architecture. There were also photographs of noted missionaries, pioneer bishops and other clergy in the collection. Here indeed was an object lesson, and in all these works was manifested a spirit of enterprise most commendable. Different countries were thus brought together in such a way as to make the student of Missions realise the fact that the Church had indeed gone into all lands and that the Gentiles were walking in the light of Him Who is the life of men. While there were important meetings held by the Auxiliary, and special services were arranged for its members, the greatest interest naturally centered in the service held in Grace Church on Thursday, October 3rd, when the United Offering for the three years ended, was laid on the Altar of God. Six clergymen gathered the alms, and bearing them to the chancel, they were received in the large gold Basin which some years ago was presented to the American Church by the Church of England. This Alms Basin is three feet in diameter, and is an object of great interest as well as value. It is used only at grand functions, such as the meetings of the General Convention. It was an occasion of great rejoicing as well as a cause for devout gratitude when the magnificent sum of one hundred and four thousand dollars was reverently placed on the Altar. Behind all this was the love which made the large offering possible, behind it too the devotion which at this most significant and inspiring service, led fully a thousand faithful women to draw nigh to their divine Lord in that blessed Eucharist which quickens the soul into newness of life. The sermon at the service of the United Offering was preached by Right Rev. Dr. Nichols, Bishop of California, from St. Luke, chapter ii, verses 22-24, and was one of remarkable power, rehearsing the righteous acts and noble deeds wrought by women in all ages.

One of the most noted meetings during the sessions of the Convention was held in Mechanics' Pavilion, on the evening of Tuesday, October 8th. It was probably the greatest gathering ever brought together on the Pacific coast in the interest of Missions or of Religion. There were not less than seven thousand persons present during the evening in the great hall, whose arches rang from time to time with applause at the sentiments of the speakers, and echoed and re-echoed the stirring missionary hymns sung by the vast multitude as led by the vested choirs of the various parishes in San Francisco. It is said that this enthusiastic gathering of all ranks was equalled only by the thousands who had assembled here only a short time before to pay honours to the memory of President McKinley, whom the people loved. Bishop Doane of Albany presided with his accustomed tact and force, and, after suitable devotions, introduced the four speakers. The first of those who addressed the assemblage was the Right Rev. Edgar Jacob, D.D., the Lord Bishop of Newcastle, who represented the Archbishop of Canterbury. He said that there were four methods of spreading the Gospel in obedience to the command of the Master, "Go, make disciples of all people of the earth." These are the evangelistic, the educational, the medical, and the magnetic. Of this last he said, "It is that the society should attract the individual. The influence of the individual must be followed by the influence of the society." Bishop Potter of New York followed in his usual happy vein. Then came the eloquent Bishop of Kyoto, Right Rev. Dr. Sidney C. Partridge, and after him Burton

Mansfield, representing the laity, who spoke about "Re-quickened Faith as necessary to all."

During the last week of the Convention there were some special reunions of colleges and theological seminaries. Among the most interesting of these, that of the Philadelphia Divinity School, with Bishop Whitaker presiding, may be mentioned, and also that of St. Stephen's College, Annandale, with its first Warden, Bishop Seymour, at the head of the table. Bishop Dudley honoured the gathering of alumni at this banquet, in the Occidental Hotel, with his presence, and Warden Lawrence T. Cole was a prominent figure.

The Convention attracted to San Francisco several well-known clergymen who, although not deputies, were nevertheless deeply interested listeners, in the galleries and on the floor of the House, during the sessions, and were also participants in services and missionary gatherings. Among these was the Rev. Dr. Lawrence T. Cole, the energetic Warden of St. Stephen's College, Annandale, N.Y., of whom we have already spoken. There was also in attendance the Rev. A. Burtis Hunter, Principal of St. Augustine's School for Coloured Students, in Raleigh, N.C. In this Church Institute Rev. Mr. Hunter and his excellent wife are doing a grand work for the negro people of the South, on lines somewhat similar to those followed by Booker T. Washington at Tuskeegee. We also noticed at the Convention and Missionary Services the Rev. William Wilmerding Moir, B.D., the zealous missionary at Lake Placid, N.Y., in the Diocese of Albany. His Missions, which have been phenomenal in their growth, are St. Eustace-by-the-Lakes and St. Hubert's-at-Newman. Under his sowing beside all waters, the

Adirondack wilderness, in the field committed to him, is blossoming as the rose. Never was missionary more indefatigable and self-denying than he, and his rich reward now is in the possession of the confidence and love of his flock. It shows what a true and beautiful life can accomplish for the Divine Master and for the souls of perishing men, when the apostolic injunction is observed to the letter, - "Let this mind be in you, which was also in Christ Jesus." This is indeed the true spirit in all missionary labours; and, thank God, it animates the Church in all its fulness, as evidenced here in San Francisco in the devising of methods for the extension of the Gospel of the Kingdom!

During the last hour of the final session of the Convention, Rev. Dr. William R. Huntington, Rector of Grace Church, New York city, a man whom every one who knows him respects and honours for his learning, his eloquence, his integrity, his character as a man, his devotion as a Clergyman, to the Church, and his love for his Divine Master, created a sensation by a speech which he made. Indeed it was dramatic in its character, and it made a profound impression on all who heard it. As he spoke, a deep silence came over the members of the House. As is well known, Dr. Huntington has for years advocated an amendment to Article X of the Constitution by which there should be given to the Bishops of the Church the spiritual oversight of congregations not in communion with the Church, allowing the Bishops to provide services for them other than those of the Book of Common Prayer. This subject was debated at length, and at last, to harmonise all interests, a Committee of Conference was appointed from both Houses. Finally the Committee reported two resolutions for adoption, - the first, that Article X of the Constitution is to be so interpreted as not restricting the authority of the Bishops, acting under the Canons of the General Convention, to provide special forms of worship; and the second, that the Bishops have the right to take under their spiritual oversight congregations of Christian people not in union with the Church, and that the use of the Book of Common Prayer is not obligetory for such congregations, but no such congregations shall be admitted into union with a Diocesan Convention until organised as a Parish and making use of the Book of Common Prayer. The first was adopted, and the second lost. Dr. Huntington then arose and moved a reconsideration of the vote on the Report of the Committee of Conference. Having made his motion, he said, with evident feeling and pathos in his voice: "I may perhaps be allowed in advocating this motion to say a single word of a personal character, or partially of a personal character. I desire to say that I entertain the same faith in the final victory of the principles which I have had the honour to advocate in three previous Conventions that I ever have entertained. Individuals may rebuke me because of too great persistency and because of too much presumeption. Great measures, if I may be pardoned in using a political phrase, may be turned down for the time. They cannot be turned down for all time. You have chosen your course for the present with reference to the great question of the opening century. I acquiesce. I resign to younger hands the torch. I surrender the leadership which has been graciously accorded me by many clerical and lay members of this House. The measure I advocated has been known as the iridescent dream. I remember who they were who said, we shall see what will become of his dream. In time they saw. But for the present it is otherwise. The Chicago-Lambeth platform has been turned down, and what I hope I may characterise without offence as the Oxford-Milwaukee platform is for the time in the ascendant. I accept the fact. My 'iridescent dream' shall disturb their dreams no more. I recall a saying of my old friend Father Fidele, whom we used to know in our college days as James Kent Stone. When he went over to Rome he wrote a book with the title, 'The Invitation Heeded,' and the best thing in it was this: 'I thank heaven that I have reached a Church where there is no longer any nervousness about the General Convention.' There is no probability, sir, of my heeding the invitation that he heeded, but henceforth I share his peace." The motion to reconsider the vote by which the first resolution of the Committee of Conference was adopted, was lost; and then Dr. Huntington retired from the House. Soon after the Bishops sent to the Deputies in Message 93, the same Resolutions as having been adopted by them, and asking the House of Deputies to concur. The motion prevailed by a large vote, and the victory came for the good Doctor, who thought he was defeated for the present, much sooner than he had expected.

The closing service of the Convention, on Thursday afternoon, October the 17th, was a memorable one. The imposing array of Bishops in their robes, the presence of the House of clerical and lay deputies, and the hundreds of San Francisco's citizens who thronged Trinity Church, together with the inspiring hymns and the reading of the Pastoral Letter by Bishop Dudley, who used his voice with great effect, made a lasting impression on all present. With the solemn benediction by Bishop Tuttle at 6:30 P.M., the great Council of 1901 was a thing of the past, but though its sessions were ended and become a matter of history, its effect could not be undervalued. It was a great advantage to the churchmen from all parts of the land to meet in San Francisco. In their journeyings from the East and other portions of the country between the Atlantic Ocean and the Rocky Mountains they had an opportunity of studying the far West, and they realised more than ever how great is the extent of the country, how inexhaustible its resources; and they were stirred up to greater missionary activity and more liberal giving. The wide domain between the Rocky Mountains and the Sierras and the rich valleys of California bordering on the Pacific Ocean, inviting enterprising agriculturalists from all sides, were indeed an object lesson. The civilisation of the West too is the civilisation of the East, and the Church, with her adaptability, is as much at home by the Golden Gate as in New York or Boston or Philadelphia. The Convention will help the Church in California. Its influences have gone out among the people in healing streams. Its character and work were a revelation to the populations by the Pacific; and already men who knew but little about the strength of our great American Church, its order, its catholicity, its aims, have been greatly enlightened and drawn to its services. They realise more and more what a mighty agency it is for good, how it promotes all that is best in our civilisation, and how it adds to the stability of the institutions of the land.

The character of the men and women whom the Church trains for citizenship and usefulness in the world is seen in two beautiful lives whose labours were finished, in God's Providence, by the waters of the Golden Gate. Mrs. Mary Abbott Emery Twing, of New York, widow of the late Rev. Dr. Twing, for many years Secretary of the Board of Missions, had travelled across the continent to be present at the meetings of the Woman's Auxiliary, of which she had been the first active Secretary. But sickness came, and after a few days she was cut down like a flower. She was a woman of a lovely character, devoted to the service of her divine Master like the Marys of old, and was a type of the tens of thousands of the Church's faithful daughters throughout the land. As she has left a holy example of missionary zeal and labour, so her good works follow her. The other life of which we speak is also an eminent example of love for God's Church, of faithfulness and good works. John I. Thompson, one of the most esteemed citizens of Troy, N.Y., though hardly in a condition physically to make the long journey to San Francisco, yet felt it his duty to be in his seat in the Convention. So he counted not his life dear unto himself, but with that sense of duty and spirit of self-sacrifice which always had characterised him he was found in his place at the opening and organising of the Convention, in Trinity Church, and answered the roll call. Exposures by the way had made inroads on his health and gradually he lost his strength until death finally claimed him on the evening of Wednesday, October the 16th. The next day the Convention passed the following resolution: "*Resolved*, That the members of this Convention have heard, with deep regret, of the death of Mr. John I. Thompson, a lay deputy of the diocese of Albany, and they hereby express their warm and tender sympathy for his family in their sore bereavement." But what a deathbed was his! What a testimony to the power of a living faith in Christ! He died as he had lived, a truly Christian man, illustrating the power of that Gospel which the General Convention is pledged to propagate and defend. With him, in the Palace Hotel, were those whom he loved best of all, his devoted wife, who had accompanied him, and his faithful son, who had hastened from the distant East to the chamber of sickness; with him too betimes the Bishop of Albany, whose tender words and loving ministrations were an unspeakable comfort to him; with him also his beloved Rector, Dr. Edgar A. Enos, of his dear St. Paul's Church, to break for him the bread of life and press the cup of salvation to his lips, and pray for him as he walked through the valley of the shadow of death, and to commend his departing soul to God. He knew he was going away from earthly scenes, and with faith and hope, he leaned on the arms of his Lord. Trained from his childhood in the ways of the divine life, and having walked like the holy men of old in the paths of righteousness, he had no fear as his feet touched the Dark River. He was ready to launch his soul's bark on the ocean of eternity. Methinks I see his purified spirit passing out through the Golden Gate yonder, but to sail over a sea more calm than the Pacific. It is eventide now, but "at evening time it shall be light;" and the light of God's eternal city is shed across his pathway as the Divine Pilot guides him through the Golden Gate of Paradise to the harbour of peace!

CHAPTER XII

THROUGH THE CITY TO THE GOLDEN GATE

A Well Equipped Fire Department - Destructive Fires - Scene at the Call Office - Loyalty to the Flag - The Blind Man and Bobby Burns - Street Scenes and Places of Interest - Market Street System - Mission Dolores - Effect of Pictures – Franciscan Missionaries - A Quaint Building - The Mosque a Model - The Presidio - The Spanish and American Reservation - Tents - Cemetery - The Cliff House - Sutro Baths - Museum - Seal Rocks - Farallones - Golden Gate - What it Recalls - Golden Poppy - John C. Fremont - Drake and the Golden Hind - A Convenient Harbour - First to Enter - With the Indians - Child of Destiny - A Vision of Greatness - Queen of the Golden Gate.

Our walks hither and thither in San Francisco will lead us to many interesting places, and at times into the midst of exciting scenes. There is an onward sweep of the current of humanity, which is exhilarating in a high degree; there is activity on all sides; and you soon catch the spirit of the place. Men have a purpose in view, something to accomplish; and there is the entire absence of lethargy; there are no drones in the great hive. You realise that you are in a city of distances as well as surprises; and wherever you go you find some object or locality or happening that calls for comment.

Hark! there is the fire alarm. The engines and hose-carts and fire ladders, with other apparatus, pass you as in the twinkling of an eye; and so skillful are the fire-laddies, and so well equipped is the department, that the devouring flames rarely ever make headway. They are quickly mastered. But it was not always so. There was a period about fifty years ago when great and destructive fires succeeded one another like a deluge and wiped out large portions of the growing city. There was then a woful lack of water, which is now most abundant, and the fire engines were very primitive in character and inadequate to the needs of the place. To-day every precaution is taken to guard against fire, and the great business blocks and the miles and miles of handsome homes are well protected.

I visited the central department, and it was most interesting to note the appliances of other days. It almost excited a smile to see the simple hand engines and old fire-extinguishers. On the walls of the "Curiosity-Shop" where these mementoes of other days were exhibited, not far from the Chinese quarter, were photographs of the members of the department, of past years; and among the faces were some of the most distinguished citizens of San Francisco. All honour to the men who protect our homes thus, who respond quickly to the fire bell which startles the ear in midnight hours, who risk their lives for the sake of others, who evince such hardihood and perform acts which are truly heroic! Some old inhabitant, if you question him, will go back to the past and tell you in graphic language about the disastrous fires which have swept over the city laying large portions of it again and again in ashes. The first, which was of consequence occurred in December 1849. Then the loss was estimated to be a million of dollars. On May 4th 1850 there was another fire which was a heavy blow to the business interests of the town. A third fire broke out in June 14th, 1850, and still another on September 17th, 1850, causing great loss. But, as the climax, came on May 3rd, 1851, what is known as "the great fire." At the time the chief engineer and many of the firemen were in Sacramento, and this greatly crippled the service. The fire-fiend held carnival for twenty-four hours, and property, valued at twenty millions of dollars, was consumed, while many of the people perished in the flames.

On Sunday, June 22nd, 1851, there was still another ruinous fire which raged among the homes on the hillsides and in the residence-districts generally. This was accompanied with a most pathetic incident. While the flames were raging around the Plaza, a man who was very sick was carried on his bed into the midst of the open place, and there while a shower of flame was rained on him and smoke blinded his eyes his spirit passed to his eternal home in the Heavens. But although San Francisco had met with all these losses in rapid succession, partly the result of incendiarism and partly by reason of a lack of fire equipment, yet the people, brave-hearted and unconquerable, rebuilt their city on broader and safer lines; and the San Francisco of to-day, so attractive and prosperous and beautiful, may be said to have risen Phoenix-like out of her ashes. So it is that evils are overruled for good in God's Providence, and the fine gold comes out of the fire of discipline, tried and precious! Our walks now will lead us up through the city to the Mission Dolores, the Presidio, and the Golden Gate. But as we proceed up Market Street we take note of some features of the life of San Francisco. Behold, here is an eager group of men and boys in front of *The Call* office. They are scanning the bulletin of the day's news from all parts of the world, which will be published in to-morrow's *Call* or in the *Chronicle* on the north side of the street. In the early part of my sojourn in this city by the Golden Gate I was impressed with this aspect of life here. It was on Thursday the 3rd day of October that I saw a crowd of men of various ages, and boys also, reaching out into the street, besieging the bulletin board of *The Call*, at the corner of Market and Third Streets. Why are they so deeply absorbed and why so interested? They are reading the news of the victory of Mr. J. Pierpont Morgan's *Columbia* over Sir Thomas Lipton's *Shamrock* in the great yacht race in New York waters, in the cup contest. Had this international race taken place outside of their own Golden Gate, on the broad Pacific, they could not have evinced greater enthusiasm and pride at the result. The pulse of San Francisco is quickened and the heart thrilled at American success on the Atlantic seaboard as much as Boston or New York is elated when it triumphs. Distance is nothing. It is America from Sandy Hook to the Golden Gate. The one thing that impresses you here in San Francisco is the intense patriotism of the people, and your own heart is warmed as you see the evidences of loyalty to the flag. I could not but be touched too at the devotion which the people everywhere displayed to the memory of President McKinley. Even in Chinatown a deep sentiment prevailed, and his draped portrait with his benignant countenance might be seen in houses and stores and in other conspicuous places.

As you walk leisurely along you will see on the sidewalk, on the south side of the street, west of the Palace Hotel and opposite No. 981, a newstand with American flags decorating its roof; and you will be interested in the man who stands in his sheltered place behind the counter on which are the daily papers. It is George M. Drum, a blind man. Poor Drum, a man about fifty years old, lost his eyesight in a premature explosion of giant powder, in a quarry near Ocean View, on the 3rd of November 1895. Yet he takes his misfortune cheerfully. He is chatty and witty and somewhat of a poet and is the author of a highly imaginative story about a "Bottomless Lake" and a "Haunted Cavern" in which that strange character, Joaquin Murietta, well known in all California mining camps fifty years ago, figures. This Joaquin Murietta has also been the theme of the "Poet of the Sierras," Joaquin Miller. Indeed it was from this "Joaquin" that Miller has taken his name Joaquin, being otherwise called Cincinnatus Heine Miller. It was my custom to purchase *The Call* and *The Chronicle* each morning from Mr. Drum; and on the second time that I saw him he said, "I wish to shake hands with you; I know you." "Who am I?" I asked, with no little surprise. Said he, "You are Bobby Burns." "Bobby Burns!" I exclaimed; and, thinking only of the Ayrshire poet, I said, "Burns is dead!" "Oh," he said, "there is a man here in San Francisco, whom I call Bobby Burns, and T thought that you were he." So the mystery was explained; and I could not but reflect that many other things which puzzle us are just as easy of solution when we have the proper key to them.

If your walk is extended into the evening through the brilliantly lighted streets, which electricity makes almost as bright as day, you will meet here and there detachments of the Salvation Army and the American Volunteers; then you will see a group of men around some temperance lecturer or street orator. You will also hear the voice of some fakir selling his fakes or wares, or some juggler who is delighting his audience with his tricks of legerdemain.

If you desire to make purchases of silver articles or gold ornaments you will go to Hammersmith and Field's at No. 36 Kearney Street; and if you wish to spend an hour pleasantly and profitably among books on all subjects, you will visit No. 1149 Market Street or 704 Mission Street. Here you will learn that books on California, whether old or new, are in great demand. Indeed all books relating to the Golden State are eagerly sought for; and if you chance to have any such you will be reluctant to part with them. They increase in value year by year.

The Club life of San Francisco is an important element; and it will be an easy matter for you to find admittance to the Pacific Union Club, the Cosmos Club, or the Bohemian Club, if you have the indorsement of a member. A letter of introduction or commendation from a clergyman or some well-known public man will secure for you the Open Sesame at any time; and here you can pass an hour pleasantly and meet the foremost men of the city, physicians, clergymen, lawyers, merchants, and army officers.

But we hasten on now to the old Mission Dolores. Let us board the street car which leads to its door. Meanwhile we have an opportunity to study what is called the Market Street system. Rumour hath it that the street railways will soon pass into the hands of a syndicate with capitalists from Baltimore at the head of it. The estimated value of the various lines is said to be over fourteen millions of dollars. These cars are excellent in service, and they climb up the hills of San Francisco with perfect ease. You feel, on some of the lines, as ascent is so steep, that the car is about to stand on end, and you cling to your seat lest you lose your balance; but you are perfectly safe. They will take you in every direction as they run through all principal streets and out to Golden Gate Park and the Cliff House as well as to distant points in the suburbs of San Francisco.

Away back in the early days of the city the Mission was reached by a plank road from the shores of the Bay; but now you ride to its doors in comfort. The Mission Dolores located in the western part of the city will always be a place of special interest. It carries you back to 1776, the same year in which the American Colonies declared themselves to be free and independent of Great Britain. The Mission was founded under the supervision of Padre Miguel Jose Serra Junipero, a native of the island of Majorca, who was born on Nov. 24th, 1713. At the age of 16 years he joined the order of St. Francis of Assisi, and in 1750 he went as a missionary to the city of Mexico. It was in 1769 that he arrived in San Diego and established its Mission. Proceeding up the coast he founded other Missions, and his desire was to name one in honour of the founder of his order. Said he to Don Jose de Galvez, the leader of the expedition from Mexico to California, "Is St. Francis to have no Mission?" The answer was, "Let him show us his port, and he shall have one." In consequence of this the San Francisco Mission was established. The solemn mass which marked its foundation was celebrated by Padres Palou, Cambon, Nocedal and Pena; and on the occasion firearms were discharged as a token of thanks to God, and also for the purpose of attracting the Indians, though it was difficult for them to understand it. The Indians were hard to win at San Francisco, but a piece of cloth, with the image of "Our Lady de Los Dolores," on it, was exhibited to them and it produced a marvellous effect. Pictures seem to have a peculiar attraction for the savage mind. In the Church of Guadaloupe, Mexico, you may see a large painting of the Mexican Virgin with Indians crowding around her. The effect of pictures is well illustrated by a scene in the ninth century, as when, in answer to the request of Bogoris, King of the Bulgarians, the Emperor Michael, of Constantinople, sent to him a painter to decorate the hall of his palace with subjects of a terrible character. It was Methodius, the monk, who was despatched to the Bulgarian court on this mission, and he took for his theme the Last Judgment as being the most terrible of all scenes. The representation of hell so alarmed the king that he cast aside his idols, and many of his subjects were converted. The Franciscans in their work both in Mexico and in California understood well the value of pictures in convincing the untutored mind. Hence it was the custom to have pictures of heaven and hell on the walls of the Missions. They were better than sermons. The name of the Mission here was at first, simply San Francisco de Asis. Then in time Dolores was added to indicate its locality, because it was west of a Laguna bordered with "Weeping Willows" or because three Indians had been seen weeping in its vicinity. Naturally the title of the Virgin would be applied to the Mission, - Nuestra Senora de Los Dolores, "Our Lady of Sorrows." In this Mission, as well as in the others, the Indians were in a certain sense slaves, as the Fathers controlled all their movements. The religious instruction was of the simplest character. The life of the convert also was somewhat childlike, in marked contrast with his experience in his savage condition. His breakfast consisted of a kind of gruel made of corn, called Atole.

The dinner was Pozoli, and the supper the same as breakfast. The Christian Indians lived in adobe huts - of which the Padres kept the keys. Some of the Missions were noted for their wealth. For example, as you may read in the Annals of San Francisco, the Mission Dolores, in its palmiest days, about the year 1825, possessed 76,000 head of cattle, 950 tame horses, 2,000 breeding mares, 84 stud of choice breed, 820 mules, 79,000 sheep, 2,000 hogs, 456 yoke of working oxen, 18,000 bushels of wheat and barley, $35,000 in merchandise and $25,000 in specie.

Such prosperity in time was fatal to the Missions. The spiritual life was deadened, and in time it might be said that Ichabod was written on them. The glory has departed. The early Franciscans were men of deep, religious fervour, self-denying and godly. They did a splendid work among the Indians in California. Father Junipero was a saintly man, full of labour, enduring hardships for Christ's sake, and he is worthy of being ranked with the saints of old. Padre Palott was a man of like character, and there were others who caught the inspiration of his life. When Junipero knew that his pilgrimage was about ended he wrote a farewell letter to his Franciscans; and then, on the 28th of August, 1784, having bade good-bye to his fellow-labourer, Padre Palou, he closed his eyes in the last sleep, and was laid to rest at San Carlos. The lives of such men make a bright spot in the early history of California; and as most of its towns and cities have San or Santa as a part of their names it is well to recall the fact that the word Saint was not unmeaning on the lips of those Franciscan Missionaries who laboured on these shores and taught the ignorant savage the way of life. On the day when Doctor Ashton and I visited the Mission Dolores we were deeply impressed with what we saw.

There stood the old building, partly overshadowed by the new edifice erected recently just north of it. Yonder were the hills, north and south and west, which from the first had looked down upon it; but the old gardens and olive trees which had surrounded it for many years were gone, and instead the eye fell on blocks of comfortable houses and streets suggestive of the new life which had taken place of the old. The bull-fights which used to take place near this spot on Sunday afternoons are things of the past happily, and the gay, moving throngs, with picturesque costume of Spanish make and Mexican hue, have forever vanished. The old graveyard with its high walls on the south side of the Church remains. Tall grass bends over the prostrate tombstones, a willow tree serves as a mourning sentinel here and there, while the odours of flowers, emblems of undying hopes, are wafted to us on the balmy air as we stand, with memories of the past rushing on the mind, and gaze silently on the scene. The building looks very quaint in the midst of the modern life which surrounds it. It is a monument of by-gone days with its adobe walls and tiled roof. Its front has in it a suggestion of an Egyptian temple. Its architecture is Spanish and Mexican and old Californian combined. You can not fail to carry away its picture in your memory, for without any effort on your part it is photographed on your mind for the remainder of your days. These old Mission buildings of California and of Mexico too are all very similar in their construction. Some have the tower which reminds you of the Minaret of a mosque. I fancy, as the idea of the Mission building with its rectangular grounds, generally walled, came from Spain, that the mosque, with its square enclosure and houses for its attendants, was its model. The Moors of Spain have left their impress behind them in architecture as well as in other things. They borrowed from Constantinople, and the City of the Golden Horn has extended its influence in one way and another over all the civilised world. But Dolores is crumbling, and its services, still held, and its "Bells," of which Bret Harte sang so sweetly years ago, can not arrest its decay. In it is seen "the dying glow of Spanish glory," which once, like a cimeter, flashed forth here. Yet, though a building fall and a nation be uprooted, "the Church of Jesus constant will remain," shedding its glory on generation after generation and beautifying the human race!

Let us now pursue our walk in a northwesterly direction to the Presidio. The descendants of the old Spanish families in San Francisco pronounce the word still in the Castilian way, with the vowels long, and the full continental sound is given. This makes the name very musical as it is syllabled on their lips. What is the Presidio? This was originally the Military Post of the Spaniards, but it is now the Military Reservation of the United States. We are carried back to the old Spanish days as we tread the well kept walks of this garrisoned post. It was on Sept. 17, 1776, as we learn that it was established. There were four of these Presidios in California, one at San Diego, the second at Santa Barbara, the third at Monterey, and the fourth here by the waters of the Golden Gate. They were built on the lines of a square, three hundred feet long on each side, and the walls were made of adobes formed of ashes and earth. Within this enclosure were the necessary buildings, of the simplest construction, such as the Commandante's house, the barracks, the store house, the shops and the jail. The government buildings as a rule were whitewashed. The chief object of the Presidios was to give protection to the Missionaries and guard them against the Indians. The full complement of soldiers in each Presidio was two hundred and fifty - but the number rarely reached as high as this. The soldiers in those early days were not, as a rule, of the highest standing. Many of them were from the dregs of the Mexican army, and among them were men sometimes who had committed crime and were in a measure in banishment.

There could be no greater contrast possible than that between the Presidio of Spanish days and the Presidio of the present time, both as to the place and the personnel of the officers and men of the garrison. As you look around you now your eyes rest on wide and handsome parade grounds, on beautiful gardens where flowers bloom in luxuriance, on groups of the Monterey Cypress, on neatly trimmed hedges, on walks in many places bordered with cannon balls, on attractive buildings which have a homelike aspect with vines climbing the walls, on barracks where the soldiers are made comfortable. The Presidio looks like a settlement in itself, and is very picturesque. I will not soon forget the beautiful, balmy afternoon, when I walked through the grounds on my way to the hills above the ocean. Here everything was suggestive of forethought, of care, of order, of dignity. The Reservation stretched out on every hand and over to the shore of the Bay northward where it has a water frontage of at least a mile and a half. In all its area it embraces a landscape, varied and undulating, of one thousand, five hundred and forty-two acres. It is a noble park in itself and well may the nation be proud of it. The Presidio was first occupied by United States troops in 1847, on March 4th, when the sword was trembling in the weak hands of Spain. On November 6th, 1850, President Millard Fillmore set these grounds apart forever as a Military Reservation. As I walked on, before me to the west, rose hundreds of tents in which were soldiers, some of whom had returned from the Philippine Islands, and others of them were soon to embark for the Orient. Yonder too is the cemetery, where, as on Arlington Heights above the Potomac, sleep the Nation's dead; and

> "There Honour comes, a pilgrim gray,
> To bless the turf that wraps their clay."

After your visit to the Presidio you will naturally desire to go to the Cliff House, that world renowned resort on Point Lobos south of the Golden Gate, and about seven miles distant from the City Hall. Thousands frequent this favoured spot annually, and especially on Saturday afternoons is it thronged. You can reach the Cliff either by the street cars going by Golden Gate Park, or by the electric railway which skirts the rocky heights of the Golden Gate. This last was our route, and the return journey was by the street railway. A Mr. Black and a Mr. Norton, two of San Francisco's prosperous business-men, were going thither also, and, seeing that we were strangers, they with true California courtesy gave us much information and showed us favours which we valued highly. As we sped westward, on our right was Fort Point just rising above tide water with its granite and brick walls and strong fortifications and powerful guns guarding the entrance to the Bay of San Francisco.

Close by the Cliff House, and north of it, are the famous Sutro Baths, always well patronised; and the lofty, vaulted building in which they are located impresses you greatly as you enter it. It stands on the shore of the sea, reaching out into the deep; and the waters, which fill the swimming pools of various depths, flow in from old ocean in all their virgin purity. Here you will find all the best equipments and conveniences of a bath house.

After bathing you may ascend to a long gallery of the building, where is a museum with a valuable collection of Indian relics and stuffed animals and archaeological specimens, and even mummies from old Egypt in their well preserved cases. The view from the heights above the Cliff House is magnificent. Almost at your feet, about two hundred and fifty yards from the shore, are the Seal Rocks rising up in their hoary forms from the sea and against whose sides the waves dash from time to time in rythmical cadence. Here are hundreds of sea-lions, young and old, basking in the sun or disporting themselves in the waters, and ever and anon you hear their roaring, reminding you that here is nature's grand aquarium. As you look northward you see the rocky shores of the ocean for miles, while to the south your eyes rest on a receding beach; and in a direct line some twenty miles westward are the Farallones or Needles, a group of seven islands consisting of barren rocks, the largest of which, comprising some two acres in area, has a spring of pure water and is surmounted by a lighthouse. Here too are vast numbers of sea-lions and wild birds of the sea, which make these islets their home, nothing daunted by the billows which roll over them in wind and storm. Surely it is a picture of the steadfast soul in the midst of commotions, when the waves of the sea of human passions "are mighty and rage horribly!" As you look out toward the Farallones, as lights and shadows fall on them, you almost imagine that they are ships from distant shores ploughing their way to the Golden Gate. But what of the Golden Gate, on which our eyes now rest? The name naturally recalls to mind the "Golden Gate" in the wall of

Theodosius, in Constantinople, with its three arches and twin, marble towers, now indeed walled up to prevent the fulfillment of a prophecy that the Christian Conqueror who is to take the city will enter through it. A similar belief prevails concerning the Golden Gate of the Temple Area in Jerusalem, which is also effectually barred. But whoever named it doubtless had in mind the "Golden Horn," that noble right arm of the Bosphorus, embracing Stamboul and its suburbs for five miles up to the "Sweet Waters of Europe." There are indeed some correspondences between the two. As the wealth of the Orient flows into the Golden Horn, the harbour of Constantinople for many centuries, so the riches of commerce, the products of great states west of the Rocky Mountains, and the treasures of the Pacific, pass through the Golden Gate. The Golden Gate too is about five miles in length, although at its entrance it is a little over a mile wide and widens out as you sail into the great Bay of which it is the outlet. This is located in latitude 37 deg. 48' north and in longitude 122 deg. 24' 32" west of Greenwich, and has a depth of thirty feet on the bar while inside of its mouth it ranges from sixty to one hundred feet. The shores are a striking feature, and on the south side range from three hundred to four hundred feet in height, while on the north the hills, in places, attain an altitude of two thousand feet; and these adamantine walls, witnesses of many a stirring event in the history of California, are clothed in green in spring-time, while in autumn they are brown, and from the distance resemble huge lions, couchant, guardians of the Gate. But who gave it its name, and why is it so called? These were my questions. Among the residents of San Francisco, whom I asked, was a Senora whose countenance plainly indicated her Spanish descent, and she said it took its name from the Golden Poppy of

California. This was the Gateway to the land of the Golden Poppy. The Poppy is called Chryseis at times, after one of the characters of Homer; and it is also known by the Spanish name, especially in the early days, Caliz de Oro, Chalice of Gold. Another designation, used by the poets, is Copa de Oro, Cup of Gold; while in Indian legends it has sometimes been styled, "Fire-Flower" and "Great Spirit Flower." It was the belief among the Indians, when they saw the people flocking for gold from all directions, that the petals of the "Great Spirit Flower," dropping year after year into the earth, had been turned into yellow gold. The Golden Poppy, the State Flower of California, blooms in great profusion and with marvellous beauty on hillside in plain and valley, in field and garden, by lake and river, from the Sierras to the shores of the Pacific, and it is especially abundant on the hills which skirt the shores of the Golden Gate. Indeed in spring time these are one mass of gold; and hence it would not require much imagination to coin the magic name by which the gateway to one of the grandest Bays in the world is known. An old Californian song well describes the beauty and luxuriance of this suggestive Flower.

> "O'er the foothills, through the meadows,
> Midst the canons' lights and shadows,
> Spreading with their amber glow,
> Lo, the golden poppies grow!
> Golden poppies, deep and hollow,
> Golden poppies, rich and mellow,
> Radiant in their robes of yellow,
> Lo, the golden poppies grow!"

The honour of having named the Gate, however, is generally conceded to General John C. Fremont. In his

"Memoirs" he says: "To this Gate I gave the name of Chrysopylae or Golden Gate, for the same reasons that the harbour of Byzantium (Constantinople) was named the Golden Horn (Chrysoceras)." It has been hinted nevertheless that Sir Francis Drake gave it its appellation; and if this be so the euphonious name would be suggested by his ship in which he sailed along this coast, the *Golden Hind.* At first the ship bore the name of *Pelican*, but at Cape Virgins, at the entrance to the Straits of Magellan, Drake changed it to the *Golden Hind*, in honour of his patron Sir Christopher Hatton, on whose coat of arms was a Golden Hind. Not without interest do we follow the fortunes of this ship. When finally she was moored in her English port after her voyages, and was put out of commission as unseaworthy, and fell into decay, though guarded with care, John Davis, the English navigator, had a chair made out of her timbers, which he presented to the University of Oxford, still guarded sacredly in the Bodleian Library. No wonder that Cowley, while sitting in it, wrote his stirring lines, and apostrophised it as "Great Relic!" How noble this thought.

> "The straits of time too narrow are for thee -
> Launch forth into an undiscovered sea,
> And steer the endless course of vast eternity;
> Take for thy sail, this verse, and for thy pilot, me!"

Had we stood on these lofty shores by the Golden Gate in the early summer of 1579 we would have descried the *Golden Hind* ploughing the waters of the Pacific northward. Her course was as far north as latitude 42 deg. on June 3rd. Owing, however, to the cold weather Drake returned southward to find a "convenient and fit harbour" for rest and refitting of the vessel; and, as one of the narrators of the voyage writes, "It pleased God to send us into a fair and good bay, with a good wind to enter the same." Was this what is known as Drake's Bay or popularly as Jack's Bay, southeast of Point los Reyes, or was it the Bay of San Francisco? Justin Winsor, in his Narrative and Critical History of America, and Hubert Howe Bancroft, in his History of California, discuss this matter in an exhaustive manner; and the reader after sifting all the evidence afforded, will still be free to form his own judgment. Some writers, wishing to give the glory to the Spaniards, arrive at conclusions hastily, though of course a name like that of Bancroft carries great weight and his arguments deserve the highest consideration. The question then is, Was the *Golden Hind* the first ship to cross the bar and pass through the Golden Gate, in the name of Queen Elizabeth of England? Or was it Juan Bautista de Ayala's ship, *San Carlos*, in August, 1775, in the name of Charles III. of Spain?

It seems to the writer that a man of Drake's discernment and perception and experience would not be likely to pass by the Golden Gate without seeing it and entering it. True, it may have been veiled in fog, such as you may see the trade winds driving into the Bay to-day often in the afternoon, but there are many hours when the Gate is clear and when it could hardly escape the notice of an experienced seaman. The intercourse of Drake with the Indians who crowned him as king, the services used on these shores out of the old Book of Common Prayer by "Master Fletcher," the *Golden Hind's* chaplain, the naming of the country Albion from its white cliffs in honour of Britain's ancient title, and the taking possession of it in the Queen's name, and many other interesting things, are all told in the old narratives, as you may find the story in Hakluyt's Collection; and most edifying is it, opening up a new world and making a romantic chapter in the early history of California. The centuries have rolled on since that time: California has become one of the brightest jewels in the crown of the Republic; San Francisco has been born and has attained greatness never dreamed of by those pioneers who laid her foundations, and before her is a grand career owing to her position and character. She is the child of destiny, with her sceptre extended over the seas which bind to her the great Orient. When John C. Calhoun was Secretary of State he laid his finger on the map where San Francisco stands now, and said: "There, when this Bay comes into our possession, will spring up the great rival of New York." Give San Francisco a history as long as that of New York, and then see what mighty force she will develop. Has she not at her feet all the great States which stretch out beyond the Rocky Mountains? Has she not the homage of all the Pacific coast lands with their untold wealth? And are not her perpetuity and greatness assured? "Whoever," says Sir Walter Raleigh, "commands the sea commands the trade of the world, and whoever commands the trade of the world commands the riches of the world, and consequently the world itself." True is it that San Francisco commands the riches of Alaska, the commerce of China and Japan, the wealth of the Sandwich Islands and of the Philippine Archipelago as well as the products of the South Seas, and what more can she desire? Her cup, a golden cup, is full to overflowing; and I see the years coming, in the visions of the future, when the city will cover, like a jewelled robe, the whole Peninsula as far south as San Jose and will embrace within her government the flourishing towns upon the beautiful shores of her great Bay. Yes, Alameda and Oakland, Berkeley and Benicia, Vallejo and Saucelito, and the villages as far north as San Rafael with all their rich fruitage, will sparkle in her diadem, and teeming millions will be enrolled within her borders rejoicing in her prosperity and her grandeur. All the advantages of Tyre and Corinth and Alexandria, of the ancient world, are her heritage without the elements of decay which led to their downfall; and if she but hold fast the principles of righteousness, which are the best bulwarks of a city or state, she will continue to reign as a queen to latest generations, sitting on her exalted throne by the Golden Gate!

Choose from Thousands of 1stWorldLibrary Classics By

Adolphus William Ward	Clemence Housman	Gabrielle E. Jackson
Aesop	Confucius	Garrett P. Serviss
Agatha Christie	Cornelis DeWitt Wilcox	Gaston Leroux
Alexander Aaronsohn	Cyril Burleigh	George Ade
Alexander Kielland	D. H. Lawrence	Geroge Bernard Shaw
Alexandre Dumas	Daniel Defoe	George Ebers
Alfred Gatty	David Garnett	George Eliot
Alfred Ollivant	Don Carlos Janes	George MacDonald
Alice Duer Miller	Donald Keyhole	George Orwell
Alice Turner Curtis	Dorothy Kilner	George Tucker
Alice Dunbar	Dougan Clark	George W. Cable
Ambrose Bierce	E. Nesbit	George Wharton James
Amelia E. Barr	E.P.Roe	Gertrude Atherton
Andrew Lang	E. Phillips Oppenheim	Grace E. King
Andrew McFarland Davis	Edgar Allan Poe	Grant Allen
Anna Sewell	Edgar Rice Burroughs	Guillermo A. Sherwell
Annie Besant	Edith Wharton	Gulielma Zollinger
Annie Hamilton Donnell	Edward J. O'Biren	Gustav Flaubert
Annie Payson Call	John Cournos	H. A. Cody
Anton Chekhov	Edwin L. Arnold	H. B. Irving
Arnold Bennett	Eleanor Atkins	H. G. Wells
Arthur Conan Doyle	Elizabeth Cleghorn	H. H. Munro
Arthur Ransome	Gaskell	H. Irving Hancock
Atticus	Elizabeth Von Arnim	H. Rider Haggard
B. M. Bower	Ellem Key	H. W. C. Davis
Basil King	Emily Dickinson	Hamilton Wright Mabie
Bayard Taylor	Erasmus W. Jones	Hans Christian Andersen
Ben Macomber	Ernie Howard Pie	Harold Avery
Booth Tarkington	Ethel Turner	Harold McGrath
Bram Stoker	Ethel Watts Mumford	Harriet Beecher Stowe
C. Collodi	Eugenie Foa	Harry Houidini
C. E. Orr	Eugene Wood	Helent Hunt Jackson
C. M. Ingleby	Evelyn Everett-Green	Helen Nicolay
Carolyn Wells	Everard Cotes	Hendy David Thoreau
Catherine Parr Traill	F. J. Cross	Henrik Ibsen
Charles A. Eastman	Federick Austin Ogg	Henry Adams
Charles Dickens	Ferdinand Ossendowski	Henry Ford
Charles Dudley Warner	Francis Bacon	Henry Frost
Charles Farrar Browne	Francis Darwin	Henry James
Charles Ives	Frances Hodgson Burnett	Henry Jones Ford
Charles Kingsley	Frank Gee Patchin	Henry Seton Merriman
Charles Lathrop Pack	Frank Harris	Henry Wadsworth
Charles Whibley	Frank Jewett Mather	Longfellow
Charles Willing Beale	Frank L. Packard	Henry W Longfellow
Charlotte M. Braeme	Frederick Trevor Hill	Herbert A. Giles
Charlotte M.Yonge	Frederick Winslow Taylor	Herbert N. Casson
Clair W. Hayes	Friedrich Kerst	Herman Hesse
Clarence Day Jr.	Friedrich Nietzsche	Homer
Clarence E. Mulford	Fyodor Dostoyevsky	Honore De Balzac

Horace Walpole	Laurence Housman	Robert Lansing
Horatio Alger, Jr.	Leo Tolstoy	Robert Michael Ballantyne
Howard Pyle	Leonid Andreyev	Robert W. Chambers
Howard R. Garis	Lewis Carroll	Rosa Nouchette Carey
Hugh Lofting	Lilian Bell	Ross Kay
Hugh Walpole	Lloyd Osbourne	Rudyard Kipling
Humphry Ward	Louis Tracy	Samuel B. Allison
Ian Maclaren	Louisa May Alcott	Samuel Hopkins Adams
Israel Abrahams	Lucy Fitch Perkins	Sarah Bernhardt
J.G.Austin	Lucy Maud Montgomery	Selma Lagerlof
J. Henri Fabre	Lydia Miller Middleton	Sherwood Anderson
J. M. Barrie	Lyndon Orr	Sigmund Freud
J. Macdonald Oxley	M. H. Adams	Standish O'Grady
J. S. Knowles	Margaret E. Sangster	Stanley Weyman
J. Storer Clouston	Margaret Vandercook	Stella Benson
Jack London	Maria Edgeworth	Stephen Crane
Jacob Abbott	Maria Thompson Daviess	Stewart Edward White
James Allen	Mariano Azuela	Stijn Streuvels
James Lane Allen	Marion Polk Angellotti	Swami Abhedananda
James Andrews	Mark Overton	Swami Parmananda
James Baldwin	Mark Twain	T. S. Ackland
James DeMille	Mary Austin	The Princess Der Ling
James Joyce	Mary Cole	Thomas A. Janvier
James Oliver Curwood	Mary Rowlandson	Thomas A Kempis
James Oppenheim	Mary Wollstonecraft Shelley	Thomas Anderton
James Otis		Thomas Bailey Aldrich
Jane Austen	Max Beerbohm	Thomas Bulfinch
Jens Peter Jacobsen	Myra Kelly	Thomas De Quincey
Jerome K. Jerome	Nathaniel Hawthrone	Thomas H. Huxley
John Burroughs	O. F. Walton	Thomas Hardy
John F. Kennedy	Oscar Wilde	Thomas More
John Gay	Owen Johnson	Thornton W. Burgess
John Glasworthy	P.G.Wodehouse	U. S. Grant
John Habberton	Paul and Mable Thorn	Valentine Williams
John Joy Bell	Paul G. Tomlinson	Victor Appleton
John Milton	Paul Severing	Virginia Woolf
John Philip Sousa	Peter B. Kyne	Walter Scott
Jonathan Swift	Plato	Washington Irving
Joseph Carey	R. Derby Holmes	Wilbur Lawton
Joseph Conrad	R. L. Stevenson	Wilkie Collins
Joseph Jacobs	Rabindranath Tagore	Willa Cather
Julian Hawthrone	Rahul Alvares	Willard F. Baker
Julies Vernes	Ralph Waldo Emmerson	William Makepeace Thackeray
Justin Huntly McCarthy	Rene Descartes	
Kakuzo Okakura	Rex E. Beach	William W. Walter
Kenneth Grahame	Richard Harding Davis	Winston Churchill
Kate Langley Bosher	Richard Jefferies	Yei Theodora Ozaki
L. A. Abbot	Robert Barr	Young E. Allison
L. T. Meade	Robert Frost	Zane Grey
L. Frank Baum	Robert Gordon Anderson	
Laura Lee Hope	Robert L. Drake	

www.ingramcontent.com/pod-product-compliance
Lightning Source LLC
Chambersburg PA
CBHW022359040426
42450CB00005B/248